HOT DOGS
&
COOL CATS
ANIMAL TALES
"A LA CARTE"

HOT DOGS & COOL CATS

Animal Tales
"A La Carte"

A COLLECTION OF ANIMAL STORIES

SERVED UP FROM W.A.G.

(WRITER'S ALLIANCE OF GEORGIA)

Copyright (C) 2012 by Writer's Alliance of Georgia

Create Space

All rights reserved. No part of this book may be reproduced or transmitted in any form or by any means, electronic or mechanical, including photocopying, recording, or by any information storage and retrieval system, without written permission from the author, except for the inclusion of brief quotations in a review.

Printed in the United States of America

Library of Congress Control Number: 1-726118581

Editor(s): Roy Berman
Cover Design by Bela Krusac and Rick Sundblad
Book Design by Donna Sundblad

First printing, March 2012

Menu

Tickle Tale Appetizers

Maggie Did It To Herself
Page 1

Executive Odor
Page 6

The Canoe-Bottom Pot-Willow
Page 11

Dog Tails
Page 14

One for the Birds
Page 19

Bessie the Basset Hound
Page 23

One Summer Day
Page 27

The Dog Who Trained Me
Page 29

Hair Trigger
Page 33

The Catfight
Page 38

Clown
Page 42

Touching Tale Soups, Salads, and Sides

Raccoon in My Washer
Page 51

Chainsaw Charlie
Page 57

A Moment of Dignity
Page 61

Ginger's Story
Page 63

I'm Adopted
Page 66

Clairvoyant Calico
Page 69

Motherly Love
Page 73

The Gentleman
Page 76

Two Sophisticated CATS
Page 83

Amazing Gracie
Page 86

Trauma Tale Entrees

Birds in My Bra
Page 96

Sasha
Page 103

Teri and the Cat
Page 106

Spitfire
Page 110

Lucky
Page 113

A Real Trooper
Page 117

Triumph Tale Desserts

The Dog that Lived Under Grandma's Bed
Page 127

Cisco
Page 132

Memphis and the Mighty Ox
Page 137

Ditto and Bogart
Page 140

Simon/Simone
Page 144

Left Behind
Page 148

Tickle Tale Appetizers

Maggie Did It To Herself
By John Leonard

The case started for me when this young dame by the name of Maggie sashayed demurely into my office. When I gave her the once over, she turned aside like she had something to hide. It piqued my curiosity, so I investigated, 'cause that's what I do. But I don't need no stinkin' badge.

Some joker messed her up pretty good. From her neck to her belly, Maggie had been colored a bright red. She didn't have to say a word. Actually, she couldn't say a word. Maggie don't speak English, only canine.

Anger coursed through my veins. This gumshoe was on the job. Finding a suspect proved easy. I started in what I believed was the vicinity of the crime scene and walked the grid. Soon I came across primary suspect numero uno.

This young shifty-looking kid named Matt looked innocent, but he had guilt written all over his face. Well, actually, he had red lipstick all over his fingers. Not the same thing as a smoking gun, but it was good enough for me.

I encouraged him to spill the beans. "Go ahead, kid. Make it easy on yourself. Confess what you've done. I'll see the Judge goes easy on you."

The kid was tough; I had to hand that to him. But I'm tougher, and I had him red-handed. Well, at least red-fingered. I pointed out the obvious, but he stunned me by his answer: "Maggie did it to herself."

Such audacity! I had to admit the kid had thrown me for a loop, didn't see that one comin. I went to confer with the boss, the Chief of Detectives, the head honcho. Sometimes, I call her Boss, but other times I call her Lisa. Or sweetie.

"Whaddya think?" I asked her.

"Beats me. You picked up the ball on this one. You run with it."

Okay, so the Chief wasn't going to be much help . I'm on my own. Maybe she knows something I don't, but she isn't talkin any more than Maggie.

I took a second run at my suspect, trying to break down his alibi. "Okay, son, you said, 'Maggie did it to herself.' But that story just isn't gonna hold water. Here's the problem. Dogs don't have opposable thumbs!"

I triumphantly towered over him. My size advantage intimidated him while I reveled in the brilliance of my logic. Surely the kid would crack under this pressure, especially after I'd just destroyed his alibi. Maggie didn't do it because she couldn't do it, see?

The kid didn't crack or even waver. He stared me down, uh, up, and repeated, "Maggie did it to herself."

He was no ordinary adversary. It became increasingly obvious; a confession would not be forthcoming. I thought it best to confer with the Judge. I didn't worry about warrants or any of that legal nonsense. I worried about crossing the Judge. Sometimes she lets me call her Lisa.

"Your honor, or sweetheart—I forget how the conversation started—this is one tough nut to crack. I need advice on how to move forward. The kid isn't confessin."

Displaying the wisdom accorded her office, the Judge asked, "Do you have any witnesses?"

Of course, I knew from experience that Maggie wasn't gonna talk. I mean, if she did, we'd have to call Ripley's Believe It or Not, because she'd be the first dog to ever speak English. I returned to scour the neighborhood, or should I say, the other bedrooms—to find out if anyone else saw anything.

I looked for a snitch named Stephanie and got lucky, caught her in her room. "Did you see Matt color on Maggie?" I knew it was a leading question, and I led her right to the answer I wanted to hear. It didn't have to stand up in a court of law, but it would have to pass scrutiny by the Judge.

"Yes." Stephanie said with no preamble. So there. I had a corroborating witness.

Judge Lisa pointed out the potential for bias in my primary witness. After all, she was Matt's big sister. She'd sell him down the river for a half hour of phone privileges or a stack of Oreo's. The judge had a point.

So I took one last shot at cracking the kid. "Son, this is your last chance. Tell the truth, and I'll put in a good word with Mom (the judge). I'll get your sentence suspended. But if you keep lying to me, I'm going to ask that she throw the book at you. I'm gonna recommend a … time out!"

I watched him visibly squirm at the threat, especially 'cause I was loud. Victory seemed within my grasp. The kid wasn't cut out for hard time. But to my surprise he stubbornly held his ground and repeated, "Maggie did it to herself."

"Okay, kid, that's it. Get in that chair in the corner, and I mean right now, mister! You don't want me to get rough with you, do you? In the chair. Now!"

"Yes, sir." He sniffed back tears as he trudged to the corner, his shoulders slumped in defeat. I stormed out of the room, angry with myself because I failed to get his confession. Under the circumstances I couldn't negotiate a more lenient sentence.

Chief of Detectives Lisa was conducting a follow up interview with Stephanie. I suspected the chief would soon accuse me of bias. After all, Judge Lisa knew all too well about Stephanie's rap sheet, which is longer than my arm. This is no household of angels we're talking about here.

"Hey, gumshoe, take a look at this."

Immediately I became suspicious, having the chief of detectives, a.k.a. judge, snooping around my case. After all, she was also the kid's mother. Maybe I was being set up as the fall guy.

When I stepped through the door and saw Lisa on her knees looking under the bed, a bad feeling settled in the pit of my stomach.

"Whatcha got, boss?" My interest interlaced with dread.

"I think there's something you've overlooked here that's gonna spring the kid." I got close to see for myself.

Sure enough, under the bed she found a telltale swath of red, about six inches long and four inches wide. I called Maggie. She slunk into the room with a guilty air, but I coaxed her with an encouraging tone of voice.

The eyeball test confirmed without a doubt, the red marks on Maggie's belly matched the smear on the carpet. The kid hadn't lied. Technically speaking, Maggie did it to herself.

Sure, he'd colored the carpet, but that wasn't the charge. He'd been accused of coloring the dog. She really colored herself as she crawled under Stephanie's bed to hide.

I shook my head in disgust. My bungling allowed a criminal mastermind to walk away, scot-free, despite his obvious guilt. No choice. I had to cut him loose. The judge was in no mood for me to charge the perp with a different count for the same basic offense. She's let me know in no uncertain terms—that would constitute double jeopardy.

So the kid walked, time served.

Executive Odor
By Rick Sundblad

I'm not quite sure how Badger got his name. Maybe because of his coloring, Badger, a tan and black Chinese Pug, had the complete package, bugged out eyes, smushed-in face, and nearly as smart as a slug. My wife and I got him in a "good deal gone bad," maybe I should say, a "bad deal gone worse." He belonged to our daughter and son-in-law, who lived with us for a while after moving from Sacramento.

Badger developed a medical problem, needed surgery, but they didn't have the extra money for the procedure. We didn't want to see Badger put down, so we offered to foot the bill. After paying for the surgery, our daughter said, "Thanks, Dad! Oh, by the way, you just bought yourself a dog." That, as they say, was just the beginning.

One thing all pet owners come to learn, every pet has their own special traits. Badger's uniqueness manifested every time he ate anything other than his dog food. No matter what he ate, if it wasn't his normal kibble, you'd swear he produced a canister of lethal gas. What filled the air smelled so bad, I thought someone pulled the cover off a septic tank. In fact, uncovering a septic tank would have been like walking past the scented candle store at the mall compared to Badger's S.B.V.D. (Silent But Very Deadly) bombs. We're talking BAD!

During one holiday season we joined four other couples for a festive progressive dinner party. A cool December evening made it perfect for such an occasion. We lived in Boca Grande, Florida, at the time, and that may have had something to do with it. We were having a wonderful time on our culinary adventure, house-to-house, then asking each other, "Whose house is next?" We enjoyed appetizers at the first stop, soup and salad at the second, side dishes at the third and the main dish at our fourth stop. The party would wrap up at our house, with dessert.

Badger, a definite people lover, ran to greet everyone as soon as they came through the door. We often joked that if a burglar broke into our house, our dog would run up and want to play. Badger made sure everyone in the dinner party received a thorough sniffing, though I'm sure not all our guests wanted one. There's something special about having a dog with a face that looks like he just ran into a wall do a sniff search on you, not to mention the eye boogers he'd leave behind. However, everyone seemed at peace with it. We started coffee perking while everyone talked about what a special evening it had turned out to be. Our dessert would be the final touch. My wife made her fancy cherry cheesecake, which she only makes for very special occasions. It's always a huge hit and this night would be no exception, a perfect end to a perfect evening ... or so we thought.

While consuming our special homemade delight, I missed the familiar jingle from Badger's dog tags. Unbeknownst to us, before the last person of our gathering came in the door, Badger slipped out. In all fairness, Badger probably needed to relieve himself, since we had been gone quite some time. We regularly let him out on his own to do his business with no problem ... unless we forgot to let him in after a short time. Then, it's anyone's guess where he'd escape to. And escape he did.

After no response to our calls, we knew it could turn out to be a long night. Everyone at the dinner party wanted to help us find Badger. "Where might he have gone?" That became the new question of the evening. Our progressive dinner party turned into a search party. Posse would be more appropriate. I could see the wanted posters:

"WANTED! BADGER - DEAD OR ALIVE! NO REWARD!"

His name began to make a little more sense.

My wife said, "We found him in front of the Temptation Restaurant the last time he wandered off."

"Well, that's right on our way home!" one couple offered. "We'll drive by there and check it out." Each husband and wife followed suit, volunteering to take a designated area of town. The hunt began.

Now one of the things Boca Grande is known for: it's a winter island vacation spot for the Bush family—I'm talking both Presidents and the Florida Governor. They came for the fishing and golf and to enjoy the holiday season in the warm Florida sun. It just so happened, the whole Bush family had arrived on the island that very week and literally took over the old inn, a favorite place for vacationers and "snow birds" to lodge. The usually quiet hotel buzzed with Secret Service personnel and Presidential staff.

The search for Badger wasn't looking good. It got late and our search party hadn't seen hide nor hair of him. We canvassed the main part of town numerous times, stopping people on the street to ask if they had seen a pug on the loose. It looked like Badger just disappeared. We decided to make one more pass around town, and, if no luck, we'd call it a night.

Slowly driving by the old inn, we noticed a handful of what were obviously Secret Service agents standing near the entrance, talking. Maybe they saw something. I decided to give it one last attempt. "You haven't seen a pug wander by, have you?" I yelled out the car window.

The men looked at each other before one turned to us and said, "Just so happens we have. Is it yours?"

After confirming the culprit as ours, the agent said, "We've got him inside. I'll get him for you."

A few minutes later the man came walking out of the inn with Badger safely in his arms. "We looked up the number on his tag. It was a California exchange. We called it anyway, but no help."

"Yeah, we'll have to get him a new one," I said. The agent handed over our escapee. "Thanks for holding on to him. Hope he wasn't a security threat."

The agent smiled, "No, we had fun with him. He's a good dog."

As we were getting in the car, the agent turned back toward us and called out, "Oh, hope you don't mind, but he looked hungry. We found some canned cat food and he seemed to enjoy it. Have a good night!"

My wife and I just looked at each other. "Thanks. You, too."

At the time, we didn't know details of the President's policy on the environment, but this we do know. The Secret Service played a big role in polluting the air of Boca Grande on one special night in December.

The Canoe-Bottom Pot-Willow
By Christy Krusac

One afternoon, following a delicious dinner after church, we went on a walk with some friends. We lived in Alpena, Michigan, near Lake Huron in an area that was rolling and rural farming country. Our group consisted of eight adults and about twelve children from toddlers to pre-teens.

The cool fall breeze grabbed our hair and scarves. Gray puffy clouds cast intermittent shadows as we tramped around farmland and wooded areas owned by one of the families. Knee-high scrub weed, tall grasses, and many bushes and hedges intertwined barbed-wire or wooden fencing that bordered the flat fallow fields, awaiting the spring planting. We stepped into openings where we could see for long distances across more pastures and fields.

Through one such opening where our group stood out in the open, a small herd of brown cows stared at us from the far end. Our talking, shouting, and laughter must have carried across the pasture. Their heads rose as they watched.

For an electric moment, human-kind connected with bovine-kind with the realization that we were all in the same field with no barrier between us. Galvanized by fear, we humans grabbed our children and darted toward the wooden fence, 30 to 50 feet behind us. After several strides, I glanced over my shoulder. Cows barreled toward us. The fence promised us safety. All of us scrambled under or over the wooden slats, handing our little kids off to each other. Helping hands grabbed others.

Gasping and dropping to our knees in relief, we looked back to see Richard, the host of our afternoon outing, still in the field. He faced the cows and performed a strange and unexplainable act.

"Richard! What are you doing?" Someone yelled at him. "Get back here!" He took off his baseball cap and put the brim into his mouth, the cap hanging open in front. Baring his teeth, he bent forward from the waist, raised his arms above his back, angled up as high as he could, and wiggled his fingers. Advancing toward the herd, he rocked from side to side with a bow-legged gait and glared, bug-eyed, standing his ground right in front of the eyes of the lead cow as the herd advanced toward him.

The bovine leader skidded to a stop. Several of the herd crashed into her and each other. Richard, never wavering, lumbered forward as he kept eye-contact with the lead cow. Stranger yet, he rolled his head side to side while making strange un-animal-like sounds. The frightened cows literally fell all over each other as they tried to turn around and get out of there. Like galloping steeds, they separated from each other and streaked to the opposite edge of the pasture. I suspect they would have kept on going, if it weren't for the hedge row.

Richard straightened, removed the cap from his mouth, and faced the group with a great big grin, followed by an elaborate bow. Coupled with the sudden relief from fear, his gesture sent us into hysterics.

We gradually quieted down, as he joined us on the other side of the fence. "I was actually portraying a dangerous and highly-feared creature of the animal kingdom, the Canoe-Bottom Pot-Willow," he said. "It never fails to instill terror into animals that go into attack mode; it shocks them into retreat. When we change our body shape into a non-human posture, especially with the big open mouth baseball cap, we appear as an alien creature to them." Richard waved his cap.

"Even animals that are normally calm around humans can sense fear, which often causes them to go on the offensive. They sensed our fear from across the pasture." Richard told us he had used this technique with aggressive dogs, but never thought it would come in handy with a herd of quiet, tame and normally friendly milking cows.

To this day I never go walking in woods without carrying or wearing a baseball cap.

Dog Tails

By Beverly Forster

    I have just an ordinary family, one husband, two sons, nice house. All we needed to complete the picture was one dog. Sounds simple.

The Search

    With this thought in mind I decided to find the perfect companion to round out our happy household. I chose to bypass pet stores and rescue a dog from the local dog pound, mistake number one. When I arrived, the gentleman told me there was only one dog available, and it would be better if I came back after the weekend. I asked to see the dog anyway, mistake number two. Not wanting to choose on my own, I decided to return after the weekend and bring my youngest son Scott with me to help make the decision.

    We arrived Monday to find at least twenty or more new strays they had rounded up. Scott noticed a black puppy, cowering in the corner, nearly hidden by all the others. He asked the man to show it to him. My son now insisted we adopt the same puppy I was warned not to consider, mistake number three. We paid the man $3.00, which brings truth to the old adage; you get what you pay for.

The Homecoming

    We took him to the local veterinarian for a check-up and shots. He also gave us a lot of advice on how to raise a puppy. Unfortunately, our dog was not listening. Arriving home, the dog introduced himself to our carport by throwing up all over everything in sight, including me. Not a very auspicious beginning, but the worst was yet to come.

The Name

After running through all the usual names like Rover, Spot, and Fido, our oldest son Michael convinced us that a black Labrador with one white paw, white chest and bald knees needed a unique name. Thus, he became Eegorre. Since he was southern born and bred, he needed a middle name. From that day forward, he became known as Eegorre Lamar Forster.

The Hurdle

My husband Steve was not enthused over our decision to add a dog to our happy home. Too soon, he said, after the loss of our first dog Pepper, the most perfect dog that ever lived. Arriving home from work, the first words out of his mouth were, "What in God's name is that?"

Eegorre was even less impressed with Steve. He bared his teeth and snarled at him, loathe at first sight.

The Test

Everything seemed to go very well during his first day in his new home. Following advice given us by our veterinarian, the task fell on me to lead him into the laundry room, put papers on the floor, and leave. I turned out the lights and went to bed.

Loud piercing screams designed to wake the dead filled the air. I acted fast. I hurried downstairs and rushed to the laundry room, where I went eyeball to eyeball with Eegorre Lamar Forster. He conveyed his thoughts. "You don't really believe I'm going to stay in a dark room on a hard floor without someone to stay with me, do you, lady?"

I explained to Eegorre quite rationally that he would never see day two in our home if he didn't shut up. He wasn't interested in threats. Okay, I picked him up and slept on the sofa. For the next two weeks he curled up against my chest, close to my heart… on the sofa

The Check-Up

The day arrived for his first check-up. Off we went. After the doctor examined him and found him healthy I decided to give him an update. "Eegorre never pays attention to anything we try to teach him."

The vet's response was to take action. He slapped Eegorre across his face and said, "This is what you do when he doesn't listen."

Eegorre immediately retaliated. His hind leg lifted and he let go, all over the vet and the floor. Not knowing what else to do, I asked, "Do you have any other suggestions?"

The vet said, "Take that damn dog back to wherever you got him and demand a refund!"

Shortly after, I heard he sold his practice and joined the army.

The Pool Fool

Eegorre firmly established himself in our home. Even though he had his downs and downs, we still loved him. Even Steve came around.

Our pool opened in May and everyone got ready to jump in. Right? Wrong! Eegorre had other ideas. Just when we thought it was safe to go back in the water, Eegorre started barking… and barking, and barking. His rules as lifeguard were simple—no running, yelling, splashing, swimming, and definitely no jumping off the diving board. In other words, stand still. If one of us decided to swim, Eegorre would jump in the water and land right on top. So much for relaxing afternoons in the pool. Well, nobody's perfect.

    Maybe my imagination, but I thought I saw more "for sale" signs in our neighborhood that summer.

Crazy Quirks
    Everyone is compulsive, one way or another. I call this "the crispy cracker caper." Eegorre loved Ritz Crackers, but when he got one, he'd take it outside and bury it. He would come back into the house, lie down in front of the sliding glass door, and make sure no one got near it. When time passed in the day, he'd go outside, dig it up, and re-plant it. Several times. When he decided to eat it… well, this part is remarkable. The cracker was always still in one piece.

    Eegorre often did his Air Dare. Whenever the air conditioner cycled off, he'd lie over the register and pant until he felt cold air. Of course, he remained in place, covered the grate with his belly, and dared us to move him. We never complained much when he refused to move. After all, he did allow us to live with him.

The Finale
I did it! I survived the first year. I don't know how, but I did. Living with Eegorre was

like reading a book, wanting to turn to the last page, and see how it ends. I don't expect to know what else our dog is capable of, but one thing is certain. I can't wait until tomorrow.

One for the Birds
By Beverly Forster

    Spring arrived with it a check from the President of the United States. He wants to give us money to spend. If the President wants us to stimulate the economy, who are we to disappoint him? Furnishing our screened-in back porch seemed like a good use of our windfall.

    With checkbook in hand, my husband sent me off to buy outdoor furniture. I rushed home after I made the selections; we tossed out all the old chairs, with the exception of a wrought iron swing I decided to keep. I don't know why—it was so hard, no one ever wanted to sit on it.

    Now I faced chores: clean windows, scrub woodwork, water down the screens, dust off the ceiling fans, run the sweeper, lift that barge and tote that bale. Working that hard made me feel like singing, "Ol' Man River." For the finishing touch I hung two wreaths I carefully packed away, the end of last summer. Circles of twigs intertwined with flowers and surrounded a watering can, one wreath, and a metal bicycle, the other. These would serve as the focal points for the new back porch.

 The furniture arrived as promised, a sofa, two chairs, two ottomans, and a table. After placing each piece, I visualized myself on the sofa, while the ceiling fan gently brushed cool air over me and my faithful dog Ginger. All was right with the world.

 The following morning, I carried my coffee to the back porch, sat on the sofa, put a pillow at my back, and meditated on the great American novel I planned to write. I had a peace and quiet moment as I sipped coffee and watched swirls of blue water dance in the pool.

 As I leaned back and closed my eyes, something touched my cheek. I flicked a small piece of straw off my face. It must have come loose from the bicycle wreath. But there was no straw on that wreath. Soon another piece of something floated down. Then I saw her. A tiny bird started building a nest, smack in the middle of one of my focal points. How dare she disturb my harmony!

 I politely asked the intruder to leave. I pointed to Ginger and explained how vicious my dog was. Ginger took one look at her and ran into the house. I then remembered she was faithful, not vicious.

 The bird ignored me, flew off the wreath and out the crawl space under the screen. Not one, but two birds returned, their beaks filled with odds and ends. I knew I lost the battle. The birds found their home and intended to stay. I would have to make adjustments in the seating arrangements. In the pecking order, I now ranked third. I got the metal swing.

    I named them Caesar and Cleo. They worked as hard as I did, building their new home in my new porch, and, before long, the nest was ready for occupancy. Cleo stayed home doing most of the work while Caesar arrived periodically to look things over, criticize, and fly away… just like a husband.

    When both birds went out one day, I stood atop the sofa and peered into their nest. I saw three speckled eggs, reminding me of Cadbury candy eggs sold at Easter. Not long after, I heard little peeps from the nest. Cleo left, so I looked again. Six little eyes stared back at me. How cool is that?

    At last. Now I could resume my rightful place on my new plush sofa, leaving the comfort of the wrought iron swing. But I overlooked something. Those babies were hungry all the time. Caesar and Cleo flew back and forth, taking care of their needs. It was sweet… until I realized the parents were not bringing toast and cereal. Instead they brought things that wiggled and strained to get loose. I retreated to my place on the wrought iron swing.

    One morning as I walked out to the porch with my coffee, I saw three fuzzy adorable baby birds ready to take on the world. They crawled up the screen, then fell; over and over, they tried. Couldn't they see there was space *under* the screen? After several attempts they figured it out. Caesar and Cleo waited for them, and, when all three were off the porch, the family of five flew off together.

I have my sofa back now and still bring my coffee out each morning. But it's just not quite the same. I miss Cleo, Caesar, and the babies. What's worse, I can't even remember what my great American novel was going to be about.

Bessie the Basset Hound
By John Leonard

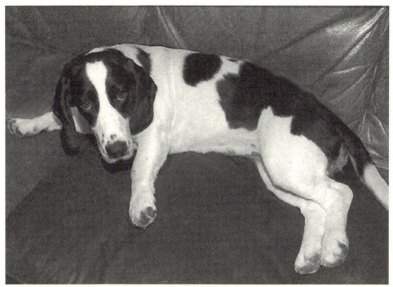

    A flash of black and white caught the corner of my eye as I drove the speed limit, a brisk forty five miles per hour. I slammed on the brakes, shifted to park, and turned to look out the passenger side window. A beautiful little basset hound trotted next to the shoulder of the road, five feet from passing traffic. Her coloring resembled a cow in miniature. I pulled over, hopped out of the van, and greeted the little dog as she approached.

    "And where do you think you're going?" I asked her. She stopped and looked up at me, tail wagging furiously. "So, are you friendly? As I reached down to pet her, she gave her reply; she lay on the ground, rolled over onto her back, and exposed her belly, as if to say, rub me. "Too bad you're shy around strangers, girl."

She wore no collar, so I coaxed her to follow me to the nearest front door. Despite the several cars in the driveway, no one answered the doorbell or my knocking. I had no means to identify the dog's owner. She was covered in fleas; I managed to pick off a tick before it burrowed into her skin. I went door to door, but no neighbor claimed the dog. She was officially lost or abandoned.

This beautiful stray could have become road kill. I decided to take the dog with me. I decided immediately, rather than turning her over to animal control—I am a volunteer with the Humane Society of Forsyth County—we took her into our program. I knew if the owners seriously tried to find their dog, they would check with animal control. We notify the county animal shelter whenever we intake a stray dog or cat, providing a description of the animal, in case the owner checks there first.

I drove to the HSFC shelter and had her scanned for a microchip, which she didn't have. The staff at the shelter gave her a round of shots, not knowing her vaccination history. I took her home, gave her a bath, and named her Bessie the Basset Hound. My wife and I have fostered so many animals over the last several years that a new name for a stray becomes hard to find. Once we'd used a name on one animal passing through our refuge, calling a new critter with a recycled name didn't seem right. We may eventually have to violate that standard when we finally run out of names, but we didn't have a problem naming Bessie the Basset Hound. She looked like a Bessie.

If we had to describe Bessie in one word, adorable would work, but sweet comes in a close second. A very gentle, affectionate animal, she blended in with our six-pack of dogs like she belonged. Bessie just didn't have a confrontational bone in her body. But no dog is perfect. Despite her gentle nature, Bessie had powerful jaws and strong teeth… and she knew how to use them.

One day an odd noise echoed through the house: Er-ER-Er-ER-Er-ER. The sound stopped for a while, but started again. Searching for its source, I found it came from Bessie, who trapped a Sponge-Bob Square Pants squeaky toy between her front paws. I recognized the sound of rubber being stretched past the breaking point, but still jumped at the loud POP! that followed.

Adorable Bessie rolled her apologetic eyes up at me and seemed very much like she emoted ? remorse. She pursed her lips. Pthew! She spat the piece of rubber she'd bitten off into the room. In that moment I learned that dogs could expectorate.

Lisa suggested Bessie would be adopted quicker if visitors to the shelter could meet her. She was right. I wanted so much to keep her, but we have a large pack, important to be able to feed and keep them all healthy. We also performed periodic dental cleanings for our older dogs, requiring anesthesia. People don't understand why the anesthetic until they envision brushing a dog's teeth against its will. But the animal's long term health includes cleaning and maintenance of their teeth. And Bessie had teeth.

After she'd been with us a couple of weeks, on this Sunday, my wife and I went to church and wanted to go out to dinner afterwards. We checked the dog pack, and let everybody out to do their business, and then we left. I made a fatal mistake, leaving Bessie unsupervised. I knew by this time that Bessie acted offended when we came and left home — again — so quickly. She expressed her displeasure on our TV remote control. Actually, Bessie obliterated it. We found its five thousand deconstructed pieces. Each of the buttons had been extracted; I got a mental picture of the dog as she spat out the numbers, one by one. How could I get angry?

    I stood over the carnage and called, "Oh, Lisa." She laughed as soon as she saw the pile of rubble. Bessie wagged her tail with enthusiasm. I tried to scold her, but my face wouldn't stay straight. Lisa didn't exactly help. When sweet Bessie flopped rolled onto her back. I knew this was an invitation to scratch her belly. She showed no sign of guilt.

    I relented soon after and agreed with Lisa to take Bessie to adoption events. Her exposure to the public shortened her tenure with us. To see her picture is to be smitten; to meet Bessie in person means falling in love. Her new human- beings have done exactly that. Re-christened Miss Daisy, our beautiful basset foster rules the roost in her new home. Occasionally we receive pictures of her, lounging in the sun or on the family couch, always ready to roll over and receive her belly rub.

One Summer Day

By Beverly Forster

One summer day, I sat on the sofa in our den. Bright sun framed white fluffy clouds in the blue skies E. L. played with his toys in the backyard.

A loud crack shattered the silence. E. L. staggered through the sliding glass doors. "What happened? Are you hurt?"

Tiny drops of blood on the carpet caught my attention. He must have been shot! I wrapped a towel around him and phoned my husband to meet us at the doctor's office. After a thorough examination, he assured us E. L. had escaped serious injury. "It looks like he might have been grazed by a bullet," the doctor said.

Ten years have gone by and memories wash over me. All the crazy things we've been through together. Like the birthday parties he loves to celebrate each year. All his friends look forward to them, too. Friends like Belle Lewis, Buddy and Susie Greeson, and Rocky King, just to name a few.

I prepare all his favorite dishes. The one most enjoyed are Hostess Twinkies, those little yellow cakes with cream centers that always feel sticky when the cellophane is removed.

I remember the year E. L. received a subscription to Sports Illustrated. He never seemed interested in anything but the swimsuit issue. When the subscription ran out he got a call to renew. He couldn't be bothered, because he never took calls while watching Animal Planet. His name must have been sold to other advertisers. American Express offered him their "Gold Card." They must have heard how special he was because the letter began "The American Express Gold Card Is Not For Everyone." How true.

I know he is spoiled, but, sometimes, we love those most who need us the most. As he grows older, he walks with a slight limp. When I retire for the night, he snuggles close to me, licks my face, and then scoots to the bottom of the bed.

I say, "Good night, Eegorre Lamar."

The spelling is unique. He is a very special dog.

The Dog Who Trained Me
By Donna Sundblad

    Black flecks sprayed across the nose of the black and white puppy thumping his tail against the carpet. He looked up with deep brown eyes. "Freckles, that's the perfect name." I scratched behind his ear. The kids loved him, and he instantly became part of the family. He climbed into the back seat of the Blazer and sat with the kids. Maybe sat isn't quite the word. He pranced from window to window, traversing laps and legs, excited to go "bye-bye in the car."
    My husband Rick and I owned a music store at that time. Freckles came bye-bye in the car every day to spend the day with us. He learned all the standard tricks, shake hands, roll over, sit, catch the snack off his nose—but our biggest challenge, teaching him to stay behind the counter. Everyone who walked in the door found him adorable. I laid a yardstick on the floor at the opening between the counter and the rest of the store, and I worked with him; in short order, he learned not to step beyond

it. Later on I removed the stick, but he'd stop where it had been, as if he'd be shocked if his toenail crossed into the forbidden zone.

At home, one of his favorite games was hide-and-seek. We'd bring him into the kitchen so he couldn't peek while the kids hid his favorite toy, a stuffed animal affectionately known as Baby. With the toy tucked away under a couch cushion or some other place, the kids would call, "Freckles, find your baby." They played for hours trying to stump the dog, but he found Baby every time.

I could tell Freckles to stay, and he stayed, even if I forgot about him. You couldn't find a more obedient dog—while he was in our presence. But it was when we weren't home that gave us some problems. We didn't see the warning signs, because Freckles went everywhere with us--, that is, until the day our lives changed ... the day we had to close our business. His world changed, and Freckles didn't understand. We went bye-bye in the car, and he had to stay home.

The problems started with drinking out of the toilet. His technique was more lap, drool, and dribble, ending with what we called *slobber mouth*. The trail of water led across the toilet seat, down the middle of the bathroom floor, and onto the carpet in the hall. We learned to close the bathroom doors before we left the house.

With his favorite watering hole closed, Freckles decided to take out the trash. What a mess. If I left one tissue in the garbage, he'd find it and tear it into little pieces. I learned, not only to close the bathroom doors, but to put the trash can up, out of his reach.

Another bad habit, Freckles slept on the sofa. With his long white hair, this had been a no-no from day one. When we returned home, he'd greet us at the door, wagging his proud tail, as if never a hair had touched the sofa, but the white blanket of dog hair and warm cushion couldn't be denied. Before we left the house, we learned to close the bathroom doors, put the trash out of reach, and prop the cushions up to keep him off the sofa.

Each time I took one of his pastimes away, he'd find another. If I left the butter on the counter, it would be gone when I got home. I pushed it all the way to the backsplash, thinking he couldn't reach it. I was almost right. If he stretched his tongue, imitating an anteater, the tip could lap it. With persistent precision, one-inch strokes gave him a greasy pleasure only a dog can love; the stick that remained was as long as a new quarter pound of butter, but half its width. I learned to put the butter back in the refrigerator before we left the house.

Once Freckles got the taste of table food—maybe I should say counter food—he scoped out the counters whenever we weren't around. On my birthday, Rick's mom brought me a birthday cake from the bakery. You guessed it. She put it on the counter, and they left the house to pick me up from the school where I worked. When we returned, all that remained were the box and a few crumbs. Rick's mother stood astounded, mouth opened and speechless. I was embarrassed. Freckles, happy everyone was home, greeted us with his tail wagging.

Freckle's antics came up in conversation on a regular basis, like salad day at the school. The participating faculty signed up to bring some form of salad. I decided to make my grandma's potato salad recipe. Time got away from me; time for bed, and I didn't have it made. I boiled the potatoes and put them in the sink to cool overnight. In the morning, I stumbled out of bed earlier than usual, and headed to make the potato salad before my shower. I poured myself a cup of coffee to help me wake up, then shuffled to the sink and stared at three potatoes. Five pounds had evaporated overnight!

"Freckles," I muttered, more like a gasp. He pranced into the kitchen, toenails clicking in his happy-to-see-me tap dance. When I showed up at work, I had to tell the teachers that the dog ate my potatoes. I'm not sure they believed me.

Every once in a while Freckles still jumped into the back seat to go bye-bye in the car. He was such a good dog ... in the car. When he had to stay home, he'd prop his front paws onto the windowsill of the picture window and watch us pull out of the driveway, his tail beating the drapes behind him with an I'm-so-cute-take-me-with-you look.

One Sunday we were running late for a pot luck dinner. We dog-proofed, bathroom doors closed, cushions up, garbage up, butter put away—and we were out the door. The car eased over the curb at the end of the driveway when my daughter said, "Freckles isn't in the window."

"My dessert!" I'd left it on the stove. We pulled up to the house and I ran into the kitchen, catching Freckles in the act. Half the pan empty, the dog curled his tail between his legs and slunk into the living room, licking blueberry filling from his jowls.

When I'd share stories of Freckles, many people thought he was a horrid pet, but he was the best dog I ever owned. His relationship with the entire family provided priceless memories. Looking back on it now, I know I could have trained him better. While I taught him to stay behind the counter at work, he did a much better job of training me on the home front.

I can just hear his conversation at the fence line with the dog next door. "My owner learned a new trick today. She stopped cluttering the counter with fruit to ripen."

"Good trick," the Boston Terrier neighbor would say. "How did you teach her that one?"

"I ate a dozen plums and almost as many peaches the other night. You know, the plums make a better snack, 'cause you can swallow them, pit and all."

Hair Trigger
By John Leonard

My wife Lisa abounds with compassion and energy. Both of our lives changed forever, the day she volunteered with our local humane society. Wanting me to experience the same joy she received from helping at the shelter, she drafted me into service. She brought a dog home for us to foster.

There is a method to the madness of running a non-profit (and non-government) animal shelter with a skeleton crew of paid staff and a complement of dedicated volunteers. Dogs deemed highly adoptable are kept at the shelter for maximum exposure to visitors, people searching the kennels for their ideal animal companion. Dogs that required special care and any overflow of strays are farmed out to foster homes.

Fostering dogs includes an inherent danger. We human beings tend to fall in love and want to keep them all. When we started fostering animals, we maintained a respectable average; two dogs lived in our house. Today we have six...or seven, if

Lisa comes home with a dog tonight. But she'll probably arrive empty handed, because she brought home a kitten yesterday.

My wife left to pick up a dog from the vet's office and drop it off at another foster home. If something happened at her destination, the dog would come back home with her. As the years passed, we became the fall-back Plan B for any foster dogs in need.

One of the first dogs Lisa ever brought home to foster was named Trigger. He proved the easiest-going dog I've ever met. If any single word best described this dog, it must be unflappable. No matter how excited or agitated the other dogs in our home became, Trigger seemed happy and grateful to be with us.

Trigger looked an overgrown beagle at first sight. Lisa described his breed as a Treeing Walker Coonhound—Trigger was actually purebred. Like all the dogs at the animal shelter, he no longer needed papers. Once neutered, an animal's credentials became irrelevant. Of course, all shelter animals are spayed or neutered, helping to reverse the trend that adds to the plethora of unwanted animals.

Otherwise a beautiful dog, Trigger had an opaque film clouding his left eye, suggesting blindness. This made him less adoptable. In his previous home, Trigger had been stuck in a yard on a chain for long periods. Given adequate food and water, he endured a lonely, solitary life with little love and attention. Trigger had some rough edges. Because of his eye injury, Lisa and I debated whether the eye should be removed. The vet said the blindness didn't appear to bother Trigger, so we decided against needless surgery. Trigger grew up a yard dog because he'd never been properly house trained. From the moment he arrived in our home, Trigger sought to mark territory for himself, lifting his leg at every opportunity, as untrained male dogs do. He succeeded the first few times.

After using half a roll of paper towels, Lisa and I introduced Trigger to our backyard. We devised a strategy to save our furniture and walls from territorial marking. Quoting

Barney Fife, "You've got to nip it in the bud." We knew we had to housebreak this dog, or he would never be appealing to a good home. Lisa researched the problem and designed the belly band. Think of a belly band as a rectangular diaper for a male dog. It is actually a cut strip of absorbent material like a towel, tied or pinned over the dog's back. The belly band, after the dog had his accident, soon became a urine-soaked irritant held close to his body, making him uncomfortable. Wearing the belly band soon taught Trigger proper indoor etiquette inside the house and protected our furniture during the training. Lisa also figured out, if the devise were tied just right, the dog would lift his leg and wet himself instead of the spot he wanted. Trigger learned to stand by the back door for us to remove the band and go outside. Problem solved.

It took time for Trigger to acclimate to indoor life. We turned on the television; it was our misfortune a music video that aired frightened him into a corner. Any loud unexpected noises, like the doorbell or the phone, startled Trigger for a few days, but he settled into a calmer routine within a week.

My fondest memory is when Trigger learned how to curl into the tightest ball possible and fall asleep in our bed, right between my wife and me. Once he wriggled into position, Trigger literally became an organic space heater. He loved human companionship, but enjoyed running with our dog pack.

Once we house trained Trigger, his popularity in our home soared. Our previous foster dogs had only been with us a week or two before someone found their bio online. We had sort of a revolving doggie-door for foster dogs. Trigger became our first house guest for an extended period of time. But he also made a distinct impression on some neighbors, causing us problems.

I vividly remember how Trigger acted toward a horse pastured on our property line. Two white horses and a red one grazed in that field during the fall months. The white mares had reasonably good manners, but red horse sought a bit of mischief.

Our German shepherd dogs were extremely territorial and took offense at their cavalier flaunting from Red Horse. He grazed right next to the fence at every opportunity, as if grass there tasted better than anywhere else in his pasture. His nonchalant manner of eating grass plucked from the very base of our fence drove my dogs insane.

Red Horse escalated. He drew the shepherds to the fence by ignoring them, then pawed, snorted, and reared up. Red galloped up and down the fence line, seemingly on purpose, like he knew he provoked the pack into a frenzy. My bad black shepherd, Ox, once got so upset, he finally broke a hole through the wire and charged the horses, chasing the three into an adjacent field. He retreated, guarding our property past the fence hole until I discovered him on the wrong side. I repaired the fence break, Red Horse regained his confidence, and the whole thing repeated.

I liked the horses but wanted to do something to make Red Horse graze away from our fence. Ox received numerous cuts and scrapes from the fence wire. Clapping my hands and shooing Red away did little good. He resisted the intimidation of squirt guns full of water and shaker cans full of beans, showing little respect for me or my dogs.

Lisa and I planned to erect a six foot wooden privacy fence between the dogs and the horses, the only solution we could think of to end the frustration. As I installed the first post, Trigger found his own unique solution. Red Horse pretended to graze right at the fence line, snorting at Ox, an invitation for the shepherd to come at him. The horse's attention focused on Ox, so he never noticed as Trigger approached.

Now Trigger had never shown interest in the horses. He approached, hiked his leg, and delivered a stream with pinpoint accuracy, a bull's eye to the middle of Red Horse's head. That got Red Horse's undivided attention; he backed up and snorted all his objections from a safe distance. Red Horse learned the hard way that Trigger didn't need to get through the fence to reach him. And the once proud horse never again approached the fence for lunch.

Trigger proved quick on the draw, able to take dead aim. We had a new sheriff in town.

The Catfight
By John Leonard

    The story you are about to hear is true. The names haven't been changed, because no one involved was innocent.

    My name is Sparky. I go to Windsor Forest Elementary School, a block from home. I'm small for my age, a bookworm, and the teacher appointed hall monitor. She makes me wear a special sash with a badge—I have to wear it every day before school starts—and told me I have to report kids who cause trouble.

    You could spell trouble C-O-L-E. My new job meant, the twice my size and in the sixth grade, Cole Hankins, hated my guts.

    He told me he'd catch me away from school and beat me up. The next day, I took my German shepherd Sheba, who's bigger than I am and my best friend, for a walk. Cole rode up on his bike and started talking trash. He didn't carry out his threat, because he was afraid of Sheba. But not so afraid he wouldn't taunt me. Cole told me if my dog wasn't there, he'd kill me. I mustered up enough false bravado to respond. "If you don't leave me alone, my dog will bite you!"

    Cole pretended he wasn't scared, but he looked like he brought a knife to a gun fight. His words sounded more confident than his voice. "You can't make your dog bite me."

    I was really afraid of Cole. I had to follow through with my threat. "Sheba, sic 'em!"

    With a short, low growl, she jumped at Cole's bike in a flash and knocked him flat on the sidewalk. That scared me as much as I thought Cole was. When I grabbed her leash and pulled her back, Cole ran away. The bully never bothered me again, during or after school.

    I knew exactly how strong and powerful Sheba could be. I was glad she didn't bite Cole, because that would have meant trouble for Sheba and me. She could have really hurt Cole if she'd bitten him as I commanded. That thought scared me.

I had a basketball court in my back yard, but we didn't play there very often. Eight different times Sheba stole the basketball after someone missed a shot. When Sheba got the ball, no one got it back. She trapped it between her front paws, clamped down with her jaws, and carried it like a trophy as we tired from chasing her. Then Sheba popped my basketball—actually, all eight of them. I can't afford to shoot hoops on my home court anymore.

One day my mom brought home a Siamese cat. Dad and I wondered if she'd gone crazy. Sheba acted like she wanted to kill the intruder, and the new cat acted like she believed Sheba meant it. With a mixed appearance of royalty and comedy, the regal cat was hopelessly cross-eyed. Mom named her Tasha, spoiled her rotten, and treated her like a queen. I wanted to warm up to her, so I offered her a small piece of my steak. She sniffed it, then turned her back on me, and raised her tail, as if insulted. Mom watched and said, "She's not going to eat that. Tasha likes her steak rare." Like I said, spoiled rotten.

Mom and Dad worked it out so Sheba and Tasha were separated and Tasha wouldn't get hurt. Our dining room, in the middle of the house, next to the kitchen, had doors on both ends. We closed the doors and checked to make sure the room was clear before letting the dog or the cat inside.

When the two animals finally met, I caused the problem, because when I checked the room for Tasha, I didn't see her. I let Sheba in with me, and we played with a tennis ball. When I talked to her, Sheba's tail beat against a dining room chair like a drummer keeping time. Tasha slept in the chair until Sheba's tail beat her in the head. The cat woke up, stretched out in slow motion, her paws behind her head. Like a flash of lightning, Tasha extended her claws, grabbed Sheba's tail, pulled it into her mouth, and bit down with a vicious snarl. One shocked shepherd, her eyes widened like she couldn't believe the cat had the nerve. Sheba didn't retaliate. The cat apparently gained some respect.

We thought of Tasha as being a little bit hopeless. Sure, she was fearless and considered herself a great squirrel hunter, but she really wasn't. Dad fed cracked pecans daily to the squirrels in the pine tree in our front yard. Tasha lay in wait at the base of the pine tree. A squirrel ran down within a few feet of her, yet managed to evade the cat and get the pecans. Dad said Tasha's crossed eyes made her see two squirrels. She didn't know which one to chase.

Summer turned into fall. When my sister and I went back to school, in our absence our dog and cat became closer friends. One day, a terrible commotion two doors away, at the neighbor's house, disturbed the peace in the neighborhood. Hisses, howls, and screeches of a catfight sounded through the walls of our house. I ran outside. Did the fight involve Tasha? Sure enough, she mixed it up with the neighbor's cat. Since she fared so poorly against the squirrel, I was sure she'd lose. I readied myself to help her. But, from what I saw, Tasha was winning. Until she quit fighting.

What was she doing? Tasha ran for dear life toward our house and into the backyard. When she reached the center of the yard she stopped, sat down with her back toward the other cat, and began to groom herself, like nothing happened. I knew our cat was not exactly normal, but had she completely lost her mind? The other cat, now recovered from her initial surprise, closed the gap between them. She sensed victory out of defeat and grew brave. All the neighbor's cat needed to show was---who was boss of the block.

The cat jumped our fence and ran toward Tasha. Our cat, still with her back turned to the advancing enemy, didn't move. I moved toward the sliding glass door to warn her, but I realized I wasn't the only one who watched with keen interest. Sheba waited patiently, as the neighbor's cat got closer and closer....

Then Sheba sprang into action. With her trademark low growl, used on Cole Hankins, the shepherd leapt to her feet in a dead run toward the feline intruder. The cat froze. For a split second, she felt three of her nine lives slip away. She was duped.

The cat retreated faster than any cat I've ever seen. Sheba's jaws snapped shut on empty air just an instant after the cat leaped for her life, just grazing the top of our fence into friendly territory. I'm sure I saw the cat's tail pass between Sheba's teeth like dental floss. My cat and dog worked as a team, setting up the neighbor's cat for an ambush, and pulled it off. The neighbor's cat never set foot in Tasha's territory again.

The unlikely duo of Sheba and Tasha proved to be a lasting friendship we never thought possible.

Clown

By Roy A. Berman

My older son Mark and I looked inside the large aviary wall at the pet store, partitioned off for different breeds of tropical birds. The owner of the store bred cockatiels in his own home. Mark, born with several birth defects, had just turned five, so this was his birthday present. He stood on one leg while holding on to his walker and studied pretty much every cockatiel in the cage. After about half an hour, the longest I had seen him stand at one time, he selected a four month old gray male, a common breed, but as long as it was a boy, he was sold on that bird. *His* bird.

After I paid half the national debt on a large suspendable cage, some bird furniture, a giant bag of mixed seeds and dried fruits, and a few toys, I packed the car. Thank goodness, I passed up the cage cover, birdie shower, and jungle gym exercise kit or I may have had to come back the next day with additional funds.

Mark sat patiently holding his new bird in a closed cardboard carrier with holes in it. He peeked and stuck fingers inside, the entire trip home. I hung the cage from a brass chain on two ceiling hooks so it swayed, something the store owner said would make the bird more comfortable. When I opened the box at the door of the cage, a gray feathered streak shot in with a barrage of squawks and wing flaps. I shut the cage door behind him. My wife Ruth, Mark and our territorial terrier Benji all served as his welcoming committee.

Mark's eyes stayed glued to the cage as his pet calmed down, checked out every corner, ate some seeds, drank water, and jumped on the swing. When he flipped upside down while gripping the perch of the swing, Mark called us into to the den to watch his bird and told us he wanted to name him Clown. Benji licked his lips when we lifted him to see into the cage, but the bird didn't pay the dog any attention. He claimed a roosting corner perch and watched all that went on from his new cool high rise condo.

    The first night Mark wanted to sleep under the cage, but Benji didn't like that. So both of them went to Mark's room, where Benji slept next to the open door, in full view of the cage in the dining area. Mark slept poorly, very concerned about his bird, but the rest of us went into dreamland — until the jungle cry woke up greater Northeast Ohio. I regretted not buying the cage cover. Benji took position under the cage and whimpered the rest of that night.

    After a month Clown lost all inhibition, if he ever had any, and showed his true character. Clown that he was, he belonged in a circus. The cockatiel learned how to open his cage door two weeks before this, but Clown set the stage this evening when he showed us *how* he could open the door at will. The cage door hooked tightly, more to keep the bird out of Benji's jaws, but the hook wasn't a problem. Clown grasped the side of the door with one foot, flipped around with his back against the door, grabbed the other "doorpost," and pushed. It gave way and flipped down on its hinges, making a great porch. I knew then, the bird would not stay in the cage. But I wondered if the Benji threat would keep Clown close to the cage, high up, maybe on curtain rods.

    His wings were not clipped, so Clown could fly from danger's jaws. And he did fly … everywhere, to every corner of the house, sat on every curtain rod, flew into windows and walls, and, because of his apparent death wish, strafed the dog from every direction without warning. The dog snapped way too late.

    We started talking to Clown, especially at meal time, as he perched on top of his cage. By the third month Mark had lost the novelty of having the bird as his pet and wouldn't clean the cage or feed him. My wife Ruth became unsettled with the bird's likelihood to nest in her hair and watch TV. My two-year-old son Rusty wasn't any help. Clown won me over, and I bonded with a bird. *My* bird was smarter than our genius terrier, who had become mine about three months after we got him. Some family trends, I've found, I could fight but never win.

Jealousy poured into our lives. I worked a full day, and Ruth didn't know any bird tricks or how to play with the dog. Clown's bold liberty inside the house proved every day he was in no way afraid of Benji. Soon the dog soon lost his desire to pounce, but not his dislike. The family entered a blood feud for my attention, the animals, my two sons, and Ruth. It was a difficult position to come home to after a hard day feuding at work.

"Do you know what *your* dog did this morning after you left?" Ruth started her evening greeting with attitude. "He got hold of my slipper and tore the ears off!"

"You don't wear your bunny slippers." I knew this was a lame defense for the dog, and it would fuel argument, but the dog clearly rebelled at a number two pet ranking, especially since he lost ground when each son was born.

Clown learned another new trick, wolf whistling, and he did it to everyone who entered the dining room. I think Mark taught him when he was bored. I burst out laughing the first time, but Ruth was still upset, walking with defiance in her bunny slippers, one with the ears missing. The situation got worse when the bird let out a perfect version of my laugh, bobbling his head as he danced on his cage. He followed with a bone-shaking jungle whoop. Benji slinked to the corner as one slipper sailed toward him. "Here! Take the other one, you mutt!" Ruth threw it and went to our room barefooted to lay down, supper half done, and two kids wanting pizza, instead. I shook my head, because the dog didn't do anything – else. When the dinner arrived, I gave Benji some of my pizza to make him feel wanted.

Mark told me the next Saturday morning, *his* bird learned to eat cereal. I envisioned the bird atop his cage, munching on a Cheerio held in one foot. We sat at breakfast with bowls of cereal and milk, and Clown flew down to join us. He perched on the edge of Mark's bowl and fished out a piece, wet with milk, and ate it. I was amazed he didn't retreat, especially when two paws slapped the edge of the table. Clown knew death was there but didn't flap or ruffle. He opted for another Cheerio. With uncanny aim, he flung it from his beak right at the dog and hit him between the eyes. Benji dropped down, sniffed at the Cheerio on the floor, ate it, and walked away, not looking back.

A year went by. Clown had become one of the family. Even Ruth had warmed up to the bird — more so than the dog. We had friends over one night and played a board game in the dining room. Clown wanted attention from us at the table, but our guests deserved our focus. We introduced the bird and then ignored him. When we sat at the table, Clown had assumed it was chow time, so he took to eating his seeds and talking to his seed cup ... loudly. Bill sat near the cage but, I thought, far enough away from the bird's space, though the entire house was the bird's space. A couple of muffled squawks made me look up. Clown climbed into his cage and jumped on his swing. The creaking didn't interfere much with our conversation. Mark went into the living room, content to play his Mario Brother's game. Russ was asleep. It took a few moments before I realized I heard Clown whistle in unison the entire sound track to Mark's game. That quickly seized everyone's attention.

"When did Clown learn the song from your game, Mark?" I wanted to know.

"I don't know. He just started singing it. I played the game all day yesterday. He sang little bits of it, then more and more. I think he knows the whole thing!" Mark beamed at his achievement and turned back to his controller.

The dog sighed, as if he knew what I felt. Bill felt something else and jerked around at the cage. "Your bird just hit me with a seed, right to my head."

We watched. Clown hopped from his swing, grabbed a sunflower seed in his beak, climbed to the roof and shook his head, letting the projectile sail right into the back of Bill's head. If I didn't see it, I'd wonder if my guest wanted to mess with me. Bill threw the seed back at the cage, because he didn't take a challenge lightly. Not from a bird. Clown countered with a wolf whistle, going into a refrain of Mario Brothers, and ended with a jungle cry a rooster would be proud of.

"You two are raising a vicious bird here. He ought to be cooked!" A smile played at the corners of Bill's mouth as he shook his head. Clown took more liberty. The next seed sailed past Bill and landed on the game board in front of his wife Sue. Ruth stood with her mouth open. I knew she was ready to scold me for not buying a cage cover, but partly because she wasn't winning.

She grew silent when Benji hopped up and rested his paws on her knee. She bent, patted him, and said, "Now you're a good dog. You're the best dog in the entire house." He tried to jump up on her lap, seeking an equal portion of attention. Benji never quite made it to her lap. We all laughed at the dog and bird show and didn't finish playing our game — the pets proved better entertainment.

My cockatiel sang his video game song and whistled every morning to each of us as we filed in for breakfast. Russ had grown to school age and Ruth finally adjusted, even hummed along. She said it was either that or go crazy with his daily repertoire. Along the way, Clown named himself Birdie. Actually, he named *everyone* Birdie. He even greeted the dog with "Hi Birdie," followed by a whoop, whistle, or his song. Several phrases augmented the bird's playlist, though I tried to believe he didn't understand what he spoke. Somewhere he learned how to whistle the fanfare of an antique car horn, and that sound clip became his favorite. From the traverse rod in the den, he listened to programs when Ruth watched hers; Clown had abandoned his desire to sit on her head.

And then the bird learned from someone, I never learned who, how to whistle for the dog. I saw it play out one Saturday afternoon, otherwise a quiet spring day. A low whistle exactly like I used to call Benji came from the cage, followed by, "Here, Birdie!" My terrier, skiddish at Clown's bravado, bowed his little head and trotted to the cage, a lemming to a cliff. A seed sailed over his head and landed on his back. The dog shook and scooted to the sofa and into my lap, where we listened to Clown's theme song interspersed by snippets of mocking laughter. Redefining the pride of a peacock, Clown mounted his cage to the roof like a conquering hero, bobbed his head, and chanted, "Birdie, Birdie, Birdie!" Not done, he took to the air and strafed my head, very close to the cringing canine in my lap, and landed on the curtain rod in front of us. I laughed loud enough to bring Ruth in from the laundry room. When I told her Clown's latest antic, she smiled and went back to washing clothes. She didn't feel the wonder of our pets like I did, but that was because they were both mine. And she told me many times, I was better trained.

   Our family saw Clown pass away 12 years later, as if we all lost one of the family. I remember his antics, his acceptance of each of us, even his war chant in the wee hours of the night. His jungle may have been the space above where we lived, but he chose to spend most of his time at human level, deeply involved with all who showed him love.

Touching Tale Soups, Salads, and Sides

Raccoon in My Washer
By Donna Sundblad

"Would you like a baby raccoon?" My sister Gail's question caught me off guard. I clasped the phone tighter. An old dream flashed through my mind, one I had as a child after reading the book *Rascal*.

"Where did you get a baby raccoon?" I hungered to know, but with two young kids, did I really need another responsibility?

"Kenny Burns raises raccoons for their pelts. He befriends one female, weans her, and, when she's old enough, lets her free to get pregnant. When her babies are born and old enough, he kills the mother and raises the babies for their pelts. He keeps a female from the litter to do it again."

My stomach turned at the story of betrayal.

"I just can't do it," Gail said. "I'm trying to take care of this raccoon, but I'm working overtime. Kenny misjudged how old the babies were, asked if I'd raise one until it got a little older. Its eyes aren't even open, yet."

I didn't hesitate. "I'll do it, but I'm not giving it back to Kenny."

"That's fine. Can you take her today?"

"Yes." My agreement slipped from my lips. *I'm saving this raccoon.*

I wasn't ready for the tiny creature Gail carried into my house. The baby slept, curled in the corner of a box in her arms. Gail ticked off a list of instructions, including a simple recipe to make formula from milk, egg, and corn syrup. She lifted the hairless critter from the security of the box; its little legs quivered mid-air as it let out a pathetic chitter-cry.

"She's hungry." Gail handed the baby to me. She fit in one palm. Her little nose nuzzled for a nipple. "She eats about every four hours. That's why I can't keep her. I'm exhausted!" Gail grabbed a small towel. "Here." She shoved it toward me. "You'll want to keep her bottom wrapped." She flashed a wicked grin and headed to the kitchen to prepare a four ounce bottle.

I studied the naked, helpless creature. It didn't even look like a raccoon. Her rounded snout, her skinny naked tail — it kind of resembled a large rodent.

The kids loved their new pet, but I let them know right away, Aero was *not* a pet. "She's a wild animal," I said. "And when she is old enough, we will have to let her go."

Chittering cries in the middle of the night pulled me out of a deep sleep. I hurried from the bed before the noise woke my husband. Downstairs, I turned on the light over the stove and settled in on the sofa with baby and bottle. Aero held the bottle with her little hands. Her pink tongue wrapped around the nipple at the corners of her mouth, her unseeing eyes trusting me to do the right thing.

By night five, I felt like the walking dead. Aero's cries grew louder, as if I didn't hear her the first time. I sat, holding the bottle, and her tiny hands held my fingers, massaged them, and suckled. Staring into her strange small face, I noticed the first hint of a mask coloring the skin around her eyes. "You *are* a raccoon," I whispered. She finished her bottle, snuggled up against my chest, inched up, and hid under my hair across the back of my neck. This became her favorite spot.

The following day I noticed dark rings shading the skin of her naked tail. Little by little, subtle changes transformed this naked creature into a baby raccoon. After two weeks, sparse fur sprouted across her back.

During the day I brought her with me most places. She became a hit at my son's pre-school. Even though my head knew she was a wild animal and would be released, without realizing it, she touched my soul and drew me in, as some animals do.

But I raised Aero to live in the wild. We made regular visits to the local park stream, a couple blocks from the house. She'd play in the running water with her tiny hands. At home I used that love of water to keep her occupied. I'd often run water in the bathroom sink and let her play, but a problem soon surfaced. When I ran water to do other things, she still wanted to play. Life got interesting. Aero became a regular shower partner; in the tub she danced behind me in the rain.

Laundry took a little longer. When I turned the knob to fill the washtub before I added soap, Aero sped down the stairs, into the laundry room, up my leg, and into the washtub. Getting a wet raccoon out of the washing machine is a story all its own.

In the kitchen I added grapes to her drinking water to keep her busy. I thought of it as the raccoon version of bobbing for apples, though she'd scoop them out with her hands. When I didn't have grapes, I'd use ice cubes. She'd pull them from the water and massage them between her clawed fingers until they disappeared. That worked as a pacifier for her busy hands, but it also developed a bad habit. If she heard ice clinking in your glass, it was her call to action. Get the ice!

Gail sat on the sofa one day sipping ice tea, the cubes sounding against the sides of her glass. In a flash Aero slipped from her hiding place under the sofa, stood on her hind legs, scooped an ice cube out of Gail's glass, and retreated a few feet away. Her hands played with the cube on the carpet, but her eyes stayed alert, ready to take her trophy and run if she had to. Gail dumped her drink in the kitchen sink.

Water and ice weren't the only things that sent Aero into hyper-drive. Her radar zoned in on chocolate, unlike anything I'd ever seen. If one of the kids had a Fudgesicle, she'd do her climb-the-leg maneuver, grab the frozen treat in her teeth, drop to the floor, and run with it. I never could tell how she knew I had chocolate, but I'd go into my bedroom on the second floor, close the door, and hide as I unwrapped a Hershey bar. The familiar sound of a 15 pound raccoon tearing up the stairs froze me in place. She stopped outside the door and started to call me. (We had this little mother-daughter call we'd do.) I stood guilty, the candy bar half unwrapped in one hand. I'd watch Aero's little hands reach beneath the door, scooping air and calling to me.

"Okay, okay." The first time, I had to share. I opened the door. Almost before I could blink, her fluffy tail end headed out the door ... with my candy bar! Lesson learned.

Life with a raccoon is never dull. When my sisters came for a visit and dared to sit on the sofa, Aero crawled from beneath the sofa, climbed up the back, behind their heads, and attacked their hair. In her mind, those animals did not belong inside her territory!

By the time she was six months old, I learned I had to have her vaccinated. I carried Aero into the vet's office. Her rump rested against my forearm while she clung to my shoulder with her arms. The vet showed concern. "I won't be liable for any physical disfigurement," he said. He had expected her to be crated.

My mind reeled. I never thought she might become vicious. He told me I should have brought help. I stroked her back. "I think she'll be okay."

I placed her on the cold steel table. The doctor readied the syringe. "It's a series of three shots," he said.

"Let's give her the first one and see how it goes." I scratched behind her ear and prayed it would work out.

The vet plunged the needle into the silver brown fur on her left hip. She didn't react; not even a twitch. The tension in the doctor's face eased, and he reached for another syringe. This time, when he sank the needle into her hip, she turned her head to look at him. I talked to her in a soothing voice and glanced at the vet. "Give her the last one."

He did. This time she looked back at his hand as if to say, *what are you doing?* But that was the extent of her reaction. She really was a gentle creature.

Gentle, but mischievous. We built an eight-foot long cage to keep her contained when we weren't home. It didn't take her long to figure out how to unlatch it. We moved it to the garage — if she escaped while we were gone, there was less chance of her doing damage, so I thought. As the winter winds blew in, Aero grew sluggish and slept in the rafters of the garage, once she got loose. That worked. I'd let her go in the spring. But spring came and I kept putting it off. I'd miss her so much.

With the warmer weather she grew more active and started getting into trouble. When she chewed through wires on my husband's motorcycle and dug a hole in the seat to remove the buttons, I knew the time had come ... in my head, anyway. But my heart didn't want to let her go. When she showed the first signs of going into heat, I had to stop being selfish. *A mate will find her and help her adjust.* I had to do it.

We climbed into the car. My husband drove while Aero and I sat in the passenger seat. We headed to Wisconsin to a no hunting area I had hand-picked for this day. Aero climbed across my shoulder to her favorite spot. A silent tear rolled down my cheek, and I turned to look out the window. Aero licked my ear as if to say everything would be okay.

We walked out to the wooded area where my youngest sister often rode her horse. Aero investigated her new surroundings without giving me a second thought. I left her some table scraps and walked away.

Back home I missed Aero at every turn. The house seemed so empty. My thoughts turned to her and I wondered if she made it. A week later, while my sister rode her horse she spotted Aero, a healthy happy raccoon. I held on to that nugget. It helped me accept the fact I'd never see her again. It's one of the hardest things I ever had to do, but if I had the chance to love on the wild side, again, I wouldn't hesitate.

Chainsaw Charlie

By Christy Krusac

Chainsaw Charlie ... what a name! What a summer!

My son and I teetered on the rocks at the bank of a brook swollen by the rain, now a raging stream. As we picked our steps, we almost stumbled over a furry brown ball the size of a teacup. I cradled it in my hands and noticed its paddle-shaped tail. We found a baby beaver.

Trudging back upstream as far as we could, we hunted for a lodge or evidence of a beaver family. Underbrush, soggy grasses, and tree trunks showed no sign of beaver activity.

My son put the infant close to his ear, heard whispery sucking noises, and told me he thought the little creature wanted food. We returned home and warmed some milk, poured it into a baby doll's bottle, and nudged the nipple against the beaver's little mouth. It licked up drops of milk and soon fell asleep.

The next day our family prepared to take our yearly vacation at a youth camp. My husband and I were employed as teachers there for the summer. I thought that the camp would be a great home for the beaver, so we lined a small box with soft rags. Our daughter and son sandwiched the cradle between them in the back seat.

As the teacher of the mammal class at camp, I volunteered to care for the little creature. He stayed with our family in the staff lodge, where I bottle-fed him every three hours, day and night. I found it challenging to care for our guest at night, opening the refrigerator door, locating the milk, pouring it into a saucepan to warm it, and wincing as it slurped on the bottle with eagerness. I was glad that none of the staff awoke because of my night feedings. With my caring for the critter along with other duties, I grew exhausted, as if I were caring for a real baby!

I called a veterinarian for pointers on caring for a beaver. He advised me to add baby cereal and infant vitamins to the milk. Soon the beaver grew into a butterball, now two hands full.

Each week's new campers were delighted with the tiny camp mascot, and soon he was dubbed "Chainsaw Charlie." This woodland pet now ruled my life. My son and I took turns carrying him around the camp like a baby, but on occasion we let him waddle along, his tail dragging a trail in the sand. Maybe because he was a wild animal, he never seemed to bond with my son or me; we always chased after him!

Charlie drew a crowd of campers every time he groomed himself. Beavers secrete waterproof oil from glands under their tails; they sit on their hind legs, use their tails as props and with their front paws, they spread the oil through their fur. Our guests found Charlie hilarious as he rubbed his paws all over his tummy, under his arms, down his torso, and around his neck. He looked like a little old man taking a shower.

Since Charlie was a water creature, I gave him daily opportunities to swim. His webbed hind feet and broad flat tail propelled him through all kinds of twists and turns, which he seemed to love. I could barely keep up. I had to grab his tail to keep him from swimming under the dock and getting away from me. When I scooped him out of the designated swimming area, I felt his fur, and, parting it, I marveled at how dry his undercoat and skin remained, because of the oil. Beavers stay warm while building their extensive dams and lodges in cold water, because this oil secretion waterproofs their skin. Other adaptations for aquatic habitat, they have watertight valves in their noses and ears to keep them from drowning. They can also see under the water through special clear eyelids.

Twice I heard Charlie slap his tail on top of the water. Beavers warn other beavers of danger by doing this, but I was never able to tell what frightened him.

Charlie grew larger, so our maintenance people constructed a partially submerged cage for him with a ramp going up to a shelter box. In a few weeks, Charlie nibbled at my fingers. I touched his mouth with aspen and birch leaves and he loved them! We fed him carrots on occasion, another food he relished. I lined his shelter box with fresh leaves and small twigs every day and loved to watch him hold the twigs and gnaw on them. Charlie's front paws have flexible fingers, which he used like human hands for packing mud and holding sticks.

The teeth of a beaver never stop growing. It can die if it doesn't grind down its incisors on a regular basis by gnawing wood. A space between the incisors and molars allows a beaver to hold limbs in its mouth as it builds dams and lodges. A special flap of skin behind its front teeth enables the beaver to keep water and wood chips out of its throat while chewing under water.

Beavers are the largest rodents in North America. Their diet in the wild includes plants, leaves, ferns, grasses, and algae. In the winter they eat the underside of bark, which keeps trees alive. They do not actually eat wood; beavers cut down small trees for their lodges.

By the end of the summer Charlie had grown to the size of a small dog. I realized I had to find a home for him. The best advice I received suggested a sheltered place for him, such as a zoo or wildlife sanctuary. But many outdoor nature centers had no room for a beaver. Others told me they are destructive to the environment. I was told their dams and lodges obstruct free-flowing streams. With no other options, I decided with great sadness to release Charlie near a colony of beaver in a neighboring county. I hoped he would be accepted by the colony and not chased away.

When my son opened the door of his cage, Charlie waddled out. He eased into the water, and never looked back, as he swam toward his new home. With tears streaming down our faces, I hoped he would live happily ever after.

A Moment of Dignity
By Amy E. Zajac

    Raining four days straight didn't stop me from the veterinarian. I had yearly exams set up for my three cats and two dogs, with adjacent appointments, so I could maneuver each of them back and forth with as little turmoil as possible. I traipsed through puddles to the car in dousing rain with two cats in their carriers, to begin the first of several trips to the vet that rainy morning. The ride through the countryside slowed me down because the drainage ditches overflowed and flooded the country roads.

    I pulled up to a stop sign. Out of the corner of my eye I saw a patch of white where the red water, stirred up from Georgia clay, surged and dashed through the weeds. A cat with a somber look lay curled up with its eyes barely opened. Red water passed through the cat's white fur. It resembled a dirty, rusty-color wet rag. With no cars behind me on the narrow road, I got out as the rain continued in a downpour. *Was it still breathing?* I placed my hand on its back. Yes, I felt movement within its cold wet body; its head moved but then settled back. With no blanket or towel to use as a wrap for the poor creature, I headed back home to retrieve what I needed. I asked my sister to come along to hold the cat in the car.

    On my way with my sister in tow, we found it at the same corner by the stop sign. The rain continued hard, and the water rushed very strong around its body. Still breathing, it offered no resistance as I picked it up. I bundled it in the towel and placed it in my sister's welcoming arms.

    As I drove to our veterinary office, I hoped to be in time to save the little animal. With open arms our veterinarian took in the cat. She reassured me with kind words but made no promises. With my sister's help, I dropped off my own two cats for their examinations, leaving them there while we made the trip back home for my dogs.

When I returned, I asked the veterinary nurse "Is my rescued friend still okay?"

"She's quiet and dryer now, but very weak. We named her Puddles, because you found her in the water at the side of the road. But we don't know yet if she'll survive."

"I'll take my cats home now and leave my dogs for their exam. Maybe when I come back to pick up the dogs, I can see Puddles for a few minutes. I'm so glad I found her and brought her here, so you can do your best to care for her." The nurse smiled and nodded.

I took off for another trip back and forth to complete the wellness day for my pet friends. My two cats, happy to be back home, ran to their quiet comfort spaces in the garage. I found my one last cat in my back porch, snuggled in a large wooden fruit bowl she made her own. I picked her up and placed her in the carrier and headed to the car.

I thought about Puddles. *One more pet in my menagerie will hardly be noticeable. I'm sure Puddles will fit right in.* I drove into the parking lot. My dogs sensed me. They barked and squealed as I approached. I hugged them, to help them calm down. After that I took my dogs out to my car while the vet examined my last cat.

I approached the nurse's desk to ask about Puddles. Her expression told me before she spoke the words, "I'm sorry. Puddles died about ten minutes ago."

My premature plans for my new little friend, died with the loss. Its tiny forlorn life ended. I brought Puddles out of the rainy, cold weather, and hoped to extend her life. Puddles died in a warm place, with good care, and with dignity; not in a water filled ditch near the lonely corner stop sign.

Ginger's Story

By Beverly Forster

Gosh, I hope it doesn't rain. I've been sitting here on this corner for such a long time. Where are they? My tail wagged with excitement when they put me in the car — I love to ride, y'know. When they opened the door, I thought they were getting out with me, but they drove off. I'm sure they'll be back, though, won't they? It's getting dark out. I can't leave because they won't find me when they come back. I'll just lie down and wait.

I must have fallen asleep. The sun is shining. I am so hungry. I'll get up and walk around and stretch my paws. Maybe there is something to eat in that garage.

Who is she? She looks like a nice lady.

The lady said, "Don't be afraid, I won't hurt you, just stay here and I'll be right back."

Maybe she'll give me something to eat. Oh boy, here she comes with some milk and cheese.

"What am I going to do with you? I can't leave you here on the curb. You could get hurt. My neighbors, Beverly and Steve, have a fenced-in back yard. I'll call them. Perhaps you can stay with them until tomorrow."

The lady picked up the phone. Sweet words fell from her lips like sugar. She hung up the phone and smiled. "They agreed to take you, as long as I pick you up, as promised."

Well, I might as well follow her. It looks like my family can't remember where they left me.

Beverly opened the gate and picked me up. "See you later," the neighbor said. *Yeah, right.*

I slept on a chaise on the back porch. Beverly brought me water and food, and I knew I would really like to stay here. The next day, she phoned all the vet's offices and asked if anyone reported a missing dog. The animal shelter told her they would hold me for 30 days. If no one claimed me, they would have to put me down. Put me down? Did that mean someone would hold me in their arms for 30 days and then put me down? Then where would I go? Beverly said, "In your dreams," and hung up.

And Steve came home. "We are not, and I repeat, we are *not* allowing another dog to train us! Or have you forgotten Eegorre? You do remember all your promises about training a dog to be obedient and well behaved, don't you? I know you always mean well, but you are not rational when it comes to dogs. I spent so much time at the vet's office with Eegorre, they wanted to put me on the payroll.

Beverly stood firm. "Eegorre had issues."

"You call $8,000 in vet bills over 10 years *issues*? You're the one with issues. You should have been the one taking him to the vet. When Eegorre sneezed, you wanted him put in intensive care. We'll try to find a home for her — and then she is gone. And that's my final word!"

The next day, Beverly said she had a plan. Every evening after dinner, Steve took me for a walk through the neighborhood. Perhaps I would recognize someone. If I did, the problem would be solved. We walked every night for days. I loved those walks, but I don't think he did. Does Beverly know Steve talks to himself a lot?

I don't know what defeated means, but that's what he said as he led me to the car. He said he had to see the vet and make sure we didn't end up with ten more puppies in the house. Oh, I'm not getting in that car. Stop pulling on my leash. I'm onto your little tricks. I don't want to go anywhere in a car. I remember the last ride I had, so I'm not budging. Why are you picking me up? Where are we going now?

The car stopped. He's pulling me toward that strange building. Who is this man in a white coat? Why am I on this table? The man's poking around in my ears and eyes ... and places a nice girl doesn't talk about.

When it was over, Steve told the white coat that I wouldn't get in the car. White coat said I was afraid of cars because no one came back for me. He suggested Steve take me for a ride every evening until I wasn't afraid. The man gave Steve a white sheet of paper, and Steve gave him lots of green paper as he muttered something about a fortune. "For what you just cost me, I guess we'll have to keep you. But joy riding with you every night is out of the question."

They are keeping me, hooray! I have a new mom and dad. Oh, oh, that car, again. I'm not getting in. I don't trust you. Oh… okay, I'm in the car but not getting out anywhere except at my new house. I'm yours, now. Remember? And another thing, I really would appreciate it if you would speak a little louder. I can't understand when you mumble.

When my new dad told my new mom what the vet said, she thought it was a great idea. Dad said, "No way."

This is now so much fun. We have been going for the nicest ride every evening. I like poking my head out the window so my ears flap in the wind. I could do this forever, but Dad gets a little testy.

"That's it," Dad told Mom. "I'm sure the neighbors think I'm weird. Haven't you noticed, no one asks us over, anymore?"

"That's fine with me," Mom said. "We'll find out soon enough who our real friends are. Love me, love my dog. But now that she's our dog, she needs a name. Can we call her Ginger, the color of her fur?"

"I think you should call her Founder." Dad said, "There's one crazy woman living in this city, and *she found her*."

"Very funny. I like my name better. Of course, she needs a middle name. Ginger Snap Forster."

"I got it right when I said, crazy woman, didn't I?"

A lot of time has passed since Beverly and Steve agreed to keep me overnight — about nine human years, I think. And I sure have loved it here. I think I'll lie on my sofa, the one Dad said used to belong to him, and think about taking my afternoon nap.

I'm Adopted
By Amy E. Zajac

I lived out in rural northwest Georgia for thirteen years, during that time I encountered many stray animals. Most of them became my pets. Every once in a while, sad as it seemed, I had to pass on adoption.

A beautiful Weimaraner dog showed up in my garage one day. He inhaled and gulped the dry cat food I kept out for my cats, as if he hadn't eaten in days. I shooed him away, didn't think much about it. Spotting him at my sister's house, eating their cat's food, I realized he was lost and hungry, not just intrusive. I told my sister and brother-in-law about the stray and we decided to take him to a rescue facility. We didn't know anyone with this kind of dog, so we take him home.

For a couple weeks I didn't see the Weimaraner, but my brother-in-law did. Several times he attempted to get the dog into his truck, to no avail. He assured me. "He's a playful canine and he likes humans. At some point he probably lived with a family. The stray appears to be purebred."

One Saturday I spent cleaning out my garage. A couple times in the morning I saw the lost dog come close to the garage opening, but, when he spotted me, he backed away and ran off. Later in the afternoon he sat near my mailbox at the end of the driveway. His stare made me curious. I walked out toward him. Maybe I could pat him. At five feet, he scampered just a few feet away, sat, and stared. When I walked away, he followed, lagging behind a few feet. I didn't understand his game, but I decided to trick him.

I went into the garage, disappointed when I saw he didn't follow me. I picked up the cat's bowl filled with dry food, took it outside to my car. The dog sat in place. I opened the back car door nearest the Weimaraner, walked around to the other side, and opened the other back door. He watched me place the bowl of food on the center of the back seat. With my body bowed and stretched inside the car, I waved my hand and talked to the dog with quiet friendly tones. He rose and came over, sniffed at my hand, and then licked it. I didn't expect such a show of friendliness. I wiggled backward, out the other side of the car.

I was surprised when the stray jumped in to eat the food, because my brother-in-law failed to catch him. I slammed the door, ran to the other side, and entrapped one barking canine. He nosed the windows while he barked. I had to admit, I was proud of myself — I caught him! I walked to the house feeling great satisfaction.

Okay, now what? Not like me to act without a plan. The dog required shelter, somewhere, but it was late Saturday afternoon. Not many places remained open. I called my vet, but, of course, they were closed. My brother-in-law came over to help, and we drove the dog to a new animal rescue facility, one I had no phone number to call.

The dog whined and jumped around the back seat, thankfully didn't try to bite us. But he wanted out! I probably should have considered bathroom breaks, especially when he was anxious as a prisoner, but this fella maintained control. We pulled into the parking lot. My brother-in-law stayed with the dog while I rushed in to talk to the employees. "I'm so glad you're still open. I've brought you a lost and very hungry Weimaraner, a stray that's been visiting my house for a couple of weeks. I coaxed him into my car and brought him here."

"I'm sorry, ma'am," the young attendant said. "The manager went home for the day. We can't take another dog without his authorization."

"But you don't understand! I can't keep him. He's too big for me to handle. Please come out, at least, to see him? He's so beautiful. I'm sure he's the type of dog your manager would accept."

My fast talking persuaded the man to see the dog. He grabbed a leash from a hook by the door and we walked out together. He took him out of the car and studied the elegant

Weimaraner. It took him only moments to agree. "I think we have a good chance to find this beautiful dog a home." I let out a sigh of relief.

As I drove away sadness and loss came over me, despite not feeling attached to the dog. Not really attached. I called the rescue facility every day for a week, asking for assurance that the rescue center didn't need to euthanize him. Busy with Christmas, I stopped calling after that.

I attended our local Christmas parade, in which scores of participants from school groups, city organizations, private businesses, and church groups marched and rode floats, waving back at onlookers. Then I saw them, the rescue group members waving to the crowd, and many dogs walking at their sides.

To my delight, the very last dog wore a billboard sign over its back. On red paper with large glittered words, it said, I'M ADOPTED. My Weimaraner friend wore a Santa's hat and garland wrapped around his neck as he regally marched along!

Clairvoyant Calico
By Béla M. Krusac

The little black, orange and white calico kitten stuck her head in an empty Pringles can and panicked. She leaned back on her haunches, lifted the can off the floor, and flopped over onto her back from the imbalanced weight. Her front paws battered the enemy as she rolled, and the can popped off. The kitten shot out of the room like a bullet and swung around the corner, waited a few seconds, and stuck her head out to see if she could spy her adversary. Neither moved. Her eyes riveted to the can as she inched around the corner. Her body twitched. With blinding speed she covered the distance and pounced with razor claws of fury, and gave the can a good thrashing. Calico darted out of the room and tore up the carpeted stairs, reveling in the joy of victory under our bed.

"This kitten is going to be fun!" I said. My wife Christy followed me up the stairs. I suspected the cat was hiding under the bed and edged my stocking foot beneath the quilt. Stopping right at her nose, I went into play mode. When I dragged my foot back, the kitten dug her claws through the toe of the sock and pinned it to the carpeted floor. I jerked my foot back a few inches, but she didn't let go; her heels anchored her in position as she tugged back with all her strength. Thus began the tug-of-wars, establishing a close man/cat relationship.

Whenever I laid lay on the sofa for a nap, Kitty would jump up and sleep on my chest. If I went for a walk in our woods, she would follow at my heels. If I pulled a sock off, like red to a bull — I saw it in her eyes — she read my mind and started another tug-of-war.

Kitty jumped up onto the bed every night when Christy turned the light off. She felt her way to my feet and curled up to sleep. Our relationship developed to the point where I swore the kitten could read my mind. A war game became intense one night. The calico jumped in the air, arched her back, flew around the corner of the room, out of sight. I stared at the corner. In seconds her head and outstretched neck peered around the wall. I made contact with her yellow iridescent eyes, which stared back. We had a stare-down and I had this thought that she smirked. I knew she wanted to play a new game. I ran to the wall, but she ducked back behind the other side. I could feel her brain waves as she waited for me. I slapped my sock around the corner without looking. Kitty's claws dug tightly into the sock and waged a blind tug-of-war with me. When she tired of the game, she ignored the slap of the sock and dashed up the stairs.

On all fours, as fast as I could go, I scampered after her and stopped just before the top step. Sensing her presence just around the corner, I knelt on the second to the top stair and slapped the sock around the wall. From her blind she grabbed the sock in a death grip. The tug-of-war continued until she grew tired. The sock went limp, Kitty jumped out of hiding spot, and stood with a regal expression of marvel and love. She blinked her eyes in affection as cats do, and I blinked back with the same demeanor. We discovered we could communicate with just a glance.

Ever after, she would wrinkle her brow, or wiggle her nose or tail while staring at me, and I would know what she wanted, food, water or play. Her eye contact and body language also signaled her time to do her business outside. On cool days she would often lie in the sun on the side deck. She'd opt for the shade of the car port on a hot day. Our wooden door began to show claw marks, so I pointed to them and told her no. Her very next outing, when she wanted back in, she didn't scratch. She stood at the door and mentally focused her thoughts, which I intercepted telepathically and opened the door. Kitty walked inside without so much as a glance, like he had expected me to open it. I was then convinced we could communicate telepathically. And I'm not alone with this belief. I searched online and found a clairvoyant cats website with others who have had the same experience.

We shared our mind link, laughed, and played together daily. Many years later, as I turned the lights off, Calico Kitty stood in the dark. I realized that she just couldn't jump up anymore. She sauntered out of our bedroom and curled up in another of her favorite places to sleep. Old age had stealthily crept up on both of us, 17 years, which meant Kitty was 119 cat years old. Dementia and feebleness came upon her, and she could not find her litter box. I could not put her down, because she still curled up at my feet, loved me, and begged to be petted.

I had to look for her one morning. She lay motionless, curled up in a dark corner by the fireplace, too weak to call for me. The candle of her 9th life flickered low. I picked her up and placed her on her pillow. Christy covered her with a light blanket. We let her sleep for most of the day and wouldn't eat. I placed a trickle of water by eyedropper on her tongue. That night we petted her, told her we loved her, and went to bed, not expecting her to live until the morning.

We turned the lights off and went to sleep. Shortly after midnight, I felt Kitty jump up on the bed like she did as a young healthy cat; the shock jolted me upright. Instantly she jumped off. The sound of her feet hitting the carpet sent a chill down my spine. I knew she had passed into the next life and had come to say good bye. I looked in the hallway, in the glow of the nightlight Calico Kitty looked back at me with a youthful expression. "Thanks for a good life." She smiled. With a final, slow blink of her eyes, she turned, and the thudding of her feet echoed in the hallway as she scampered down the stairs. I looked at the clock. 12:10 glowed green. Dragging myself out of bed, I went down stairs. Kitty's lifeless form lay still warm on the pillow. She had left her body behind, said goodbye, and went to a better place.

Motherly Love
By Amy E. Zajac

Moving to California fulfilled a lifelong dream for my parents in 1977. They moved into a new stucco Spanish hacienda. Mom enjoyed her daily exercise, landscaping a new yard. After working diligently for two years, healthy and colorful flora caught up with other neighborhood homes and the city's tree planting. She was proud of her prize courtyard built in the center of the house. Hedges, exotic Birds of Paradise, a special palm, and a miniature Crape Myrtle captured a mood of comfort and warmth as visitors walked through to the front door.

When workmen cut down trees planted by the city along my mother's street, she investigated. The city's plan had directed them to cut down all the diseased trees. She expressed her concern to the foreman about a hummingbird nest in front of her house. "I know you're just doing your job, but would you please consider these tiny recently hatched birds?" Gesturing to come closer to a particular tree, she said, "See the two beaks pointing out of the nest. These babies are so tiny and innocent. If you cut down the tree, their mother will not be able to save them, and they will die."

"We can't save the tree," the foreman said. "The blight spread, so the tree needs to be eliminated. I have my orders, no exceptions."

Mom became frustrated as the foreman held his ground. She returned to the house. As the sound of the trucks got closer, Mom went back outside. Anxiety grew in the pit of her stomach. *How can I help these creatures?* She saw the foreman approach, carrying a large branch. "I thought over what you said, and I didn't want you to be upset with our crew not caring about our local wild life. I cut out the branch for you." He pointed. "Look. You can see the bird's nest lodged right here." He handed the branch to my mother.

Mom expressed her gratitude as he left. *Now what will I do with them? Their mother won't be able to care for them again. These babies will be lost to her.*

She carried the branch toward the house. The trees in her front yard weren't big enough to attach this branch to them, but the Crape Myrtle in the courtyard could hold it. She slid the cut branch between two large tree limbs and allowed it to settle backwards into place. Binding it to the main tree with a length of rope, she called her veterinarian to ask advice. The vet delivered bad news; the babies would not survive.

Mom prepared a glass eye dropper to give them milk mixed with warm water. She didn't know if the birds would drink it or if they would get sick. When she walked outside, she was surprised. The mother hummingbird flew in circles inside the courtyard; she found her babies. Mom backtracked into the house and looked out the window. The mother hummingbird flew into the tree and perched on the edge of the nest, communicating with her babies. The knot in Mom's stomach unraveled, but she couldn't believe her eyes.

During the following few weeks, the baby birds flourished in their mother's care. One morning, the tiny birds stood side by side on the edge of their nest. The next day, as Mom went in and out of the house through the courtyard, the baby birds flew in front of her path. With a human so close by, the new flyers became startled and flew away from their nest instead of to it. They landed on the farthest inside wall of the courtyard and clung to the stucco with their tiny feet. Their first giant step to fly sent them in the wrong direction.

Mom watched the baby birds, who would not return to their nest. They clung to the stucco and remained motionless. Their mother flew through a couple times, yet still they did not take flight. After an hour Mom approached the outside courtyard wall. With slow deliberate movements, remaining as invisible to them as possible, Mom reached out and captured the first baby. Holding it with as tender a grip as possible, she took it to the nest. Mom repeated the action for the second baby. *I don't really know if the hummingbird mother will feed and help the babies learn how to fly.* Returning to the house, Mom stood in vigil at the window. A half hour went by. No sign of the mother. Anxiety grabbed at my Mom's heartstrings. *By touching the babies, I took a chance that their mother would abandon them, but what else could I do?* By returning the baby birds back to their nest, Mom believed she caused a problem, because she startled the new flyers when she walked through the courtyard. But she refused to give up on them.

Later that evening, Mom's hope for saving the young birds bore fruit. The mother hummingbird returned to the nest and fed them. Their tiny beaks outstretched, they reached for the food. The human scent on her babies didn't deter her from her daily task of motherly love.

The Gentleman

By Angie Kinsey

I grabbed the keys to our car my two kids, Jeff and Shelly, nick-named 'the banana boat'. As I headed to the door to get Shelly's prescription, Jeff, just three, clung to my leg and looked up at me, "Mom, please don't leave me here alone."

I hugged Jeff and put my hands on his shoulders, "I'll be back soon. You're not alone. Grandma will take good care of you. Shelly's here, too, and she needs her medicine."

Jeff took a step back and rubbed his tiny hands together as he often did when he was uneasy. "Because of the operation? Is Shelly going to be okay?"

I pulled Jeff close to me, "Yes, baby. Shelly will be just fine. The doctors fixed her. She just needs her medicine to make sure she stays well."

Shelly, 18 months old, toddled toward me, "Mama, can I go?"

I picked her up and pointed to the bandage on her stomach. "No, Shelly. You're boo-boo is better, but you have to stay here with Grandma while I get your medicine." Shelly kissed me on the cheek. As I put her down, waved good-bye, walked out the door, the jagged edge of a tear in the screen caught my coat and ripped my sleeve. I wriggled free. I cursed under my breath, and said, "Please God, just a little help here? I'm not asking for much. Just a little. Please?"

I dropped off the prescription. The pharmacist looked up for a moment, "It'll be about twenty minutes." I browsed the products on the shelves. I paced back and forth in the isles. I thought about Jeff wringing his hands, and about leaving Shelly for the first time since her operation. I felt hot and nauseas. The walls of the pharmacy seemed to be closing in on me. I went outside to get some air. I sat alone on a bench. A paper fluttered past me in the wind. When I picked it up, I noticed a red circle drawn around an ad about a full-blooded miniature schnauzer puppy for sale. I couldn't believe the dog was within our price range. I got the prescription, but my thoughts swirled around the puppy all the way home. The dog would probably be taken long before I could call the seller.

After I tucked them in, I made the call.

"Do you still have a puppy for sale?"

"Yes. We do," the dog owner said, "but I should explain. We want the puppy to go to a good home, preferably with small children."

"Wow. That's great." I smiled. The lady intended to keep the dog as a pet, but changed her mind. She simply wanted a good home for him and children for him to play with. We agreed to meet at a restaurant the next day.

I went alone, in case the dog was not suitable for us. When I got to the restaurant, I saw a blonde woman holding a small puppy. The dog was gray, scruffy, had bushy salt and pepper eyebrows, a stubby little tail, and a white beard. I reached out to hold him, and he jumped into my arms. "Looks like we have a match!" The lady laughed, so I joined in clutching an arm full of curls.

I brought him home. I asked the children to cover their eyes while I retrieved the dog from the car. Shelly and her brother stood beside the aquarium where Moby-Dick ruled the seas, eyes squeezed shut. "Uncover your eyes!" I put the puppy on the floor, and he immediately started barking up at the goldfish. The sound of his bark boomed through the house, and startled us, more than the fish, "Such a big bark from such a small dog." The dog inched closer to the aquarium and barked again. The kids laughed. With each bark and belly laugh, the tension began to evaporate. The dog quieted down, and the children circled him with excitement and patted him all over.

Jeff decided to name the dog Max after the character in a children's book that roars at the wild things.

I bought puppy food, a doggy bed, and a collar for Max. Shelly and Jeff built tent-forts. and played tug-of-war until they were exhausted. They slipped Max food under the table while I pretended not to notice.

Max began to develop character, and organized a bedtime routine. He made his rounds like an orderly and napped on his doggy bed until the children went to sleep. He would rise, creep down the hall into Shelly's room, jump on the bed, and sniff her. Max moved stealthily down the hall to Jeff's room, hopped up on his bed, sniffed his hair, and nestled into bed with him for the night. In the early morning hours, Max snuck back up the hallway into my room to sleep at the foot of my bed.

One day, I heard giggling, rapid footsteps, and scraping against the tile. When I went to investigate, I couldn't believe my eyes. Max bit down on Shelly's diaper as she dragged him through the house as fast as she could. Max growled as he struggled to hang on to the diaper while she twisted, turned, and ran. Jeff cheered them on and squealed with laughter.

Shelly's potty training was going well, and she gained encouragement by helping me house-train Max. She escorted him to the door, pointed, and said, "See Max, you potty outside. I potty inside." They both had occasional accidents, but they were comrades.

One day, when I went to check on Shelly in the bathroom, I stepped in a puddle. Max stood near the bathroom door just beyond the puddle. He cowered, and I picked him up by the scruff of the neck. "Bad dog!"

Shelly flung open the bathroom door, "Put him down, Mama." As I put the dog on the floor, Max exhaled sharply, raised one eyebrow, and sat back on his haunches. Shelly took her place next to Max and said, "It's not Max, Mama. I couldn't get to the bathroom." Shelly turned around and went back into the bathroom. Max raised his head in the air, huffed, cocked one eyebrow, turned, and trotted behind Shelly. I was left to clean up the puddle.

The days grew longer with the onset of spring and sunny summer days were plentiful. The children played outside with Max, and before I knew it, Shelly had a golden brown color back in her skin. They threw sticks for Max to retrieve, and he brought them presents of bugs and dead rodents. They regularly chased each other around the yard until I made them come in for dinner.

One evening as bedtime approached, Jeff and I watched TV. Shelly and Max scuffled on the floor. Shelly stopped for a moment. Max faced me, and Shelly was behind him. Shelly squinted her eyes, and Max let out a strained yelp. Shelly said, "Chocolate." I darted across the room, and grabbed Shelly's hand.

Jeff yelled, "Gross!"

I explained to Shelly that the dog was not hiding chocolate anywhere in or on his body. Jeff laughed so hard he cried. Max hid underneath the sofa until Shelly went to bed.

The event left Max protective of his flank, but it didn't stop him from playing with the children, or from becoming my informant.

One day Max barked at me until I followed him into the bathroom where the children were playing with the bathroom cleanser. Shelly was completely naked in the tub with her hands, knees, and feet in the pasty mixture. Jeff poured water into the tub with his toothbrush-rinse cup. Shelly yelled, "Cold."

Jeff smiled and said, "We're cleaning the tub, Mama." Max sat down next to me and puffed. "Why does he do that Mama?"

I grabbed my rubber gloves and pulled Shelly out of the tub to wash her off. "He's expressing his displeasure." Jeff squinted at me. "Max doesn't like what you two are doing." Jeff looked at the floor and sighed.

When Jeff climbed his first tree, despite my warnings, Max barked continuously until I came to the door to see what Jeff had done. "Jeff, get down from there." I went to the tree to help him down, and Max followed closely behind me. Jeff locked eyes with Max. "Tattle-tale."

Max was like an early warning system for children.

After the kids were safely tucked into bed one night, Max made his rounds. He traveled from Shelly's room, to Jeff's room, and immediately came into my room. He barked at me, and I told him to be quiet. Max jumped onto my bed and barked. I rolled over, and he pounced on my head and started digging at my hair. I got up, "Dog, what is your problem!?" He whined, hopped off the bed, barked again, and headed toward my bedroom door. I got up and went to the front door to let him outside, but he refused to go. He barked at me again, cocked his eyebrow, and then exhaled sharply. I shut the front door, and he took off like a shot down the hallway toward Jeff's room. He spun and came right back to me.

"What is it?"

Max ran halfway down the hallway that led to Jeff's room and barked again.

"Is it Jeff?"

The dog barked desperately and ran into Jeff's room. Max used his paws to dig at Jeff's blonde hair. "Leave him alone, Max." I tried to sweep him away, but the dog chomped down on my sleeve. I wrenched my sleeve free of him, but he snatched it again, pulling me closer to Jeff. The child was burning up. I went to get the thermometer, and Max stood over him silently until I returned. I took Jeff's temperature. It was over 104 degrees. I called the doctor who told me to get him to the ER right away. Max watched quietly as I bundled Jeff up, and took him to the car.

According to the doctor, Jeff had a serious infection, and I brought him in just in time for treatment. Four years later, it would be Jeff who found Max lying lifeless at the foot of his bed. Jeff came into my room and said, "Mom, I think there's something wrong with Max." Jeff took me to his room where Max did not respond. His eyes were closed, and his nose was hot. I called the vet. He told me to bring Max to his office right away.

Max stayed three days for intravenous feeding and antibiotics. During that time, the children constantly asked me, "Will Max be okay?"

"I hope so." Finally, the vet called to tell us we could pick him up. When we put Max in the car, he was still recovering from a nasty infection, slow-moving, but he managed a few nuzzles and nudges for each child, and wagged his stubbed-tail.

"He's going be okay. Isn't he?" Shelly said. "Why didn't Max let us know he was sick, Mom?"

I thought for a moment, "Because he's a gentleman, Shelly, and gentlemen never worry their women needlessly." Shelly smiled and tussled Max's hair.

As the years rolled by, the children grew into new things, but never outgrew Max. They confided in him when they felt they couldn't confide in me. They played with Max when no one else was around, or when they didn't want anyone else around. He was a best-friend, a confidant, an entertainment center, the sentinel they counted on to watch over them in the night, my trusted partner in caring for them, and, at times, my only friend.

One November morning, when both Max and I moved at a much slower pace, he pounced onto my bed like the puppy I had brought home 15 years earlier. He licked my face, rolled over onto his arthritic back, and let me give him a belly-rub. Strangely, he popped up on all fours and looked at me, staring straight into my eyes. He stood completely frozen for a few minutes. I whispered, "I love you, Max," and the spell was broken. He wagged his stubby-tail, exhaled softly, licked my face, and jumped off the bed. He started toward the door, turned around, lingered for one moment more, pattered out of my room, and went outside through the doggy door.

    That afternoon, when the children, now teenagers, came home from school, they couldn't find Max. We called his name, shook his favorite treat bag, but there was no response. An eerie feeling came over me. I asked the children to stay inside. I put on my boots, and went outside to look for Max. I walked around the property calling his name for a long while. After I crossed the barbed-wire fence in the backyard, I found Max lying lifeless on a tuft of dried grass. As I stared down at his lifeless body, it occurred to me that he lived a trouble-free life and died a trouble-free death. Tears poured down my face. As I reached down to touch him, I realized Max had even taken the time to say 'Good-bye' to me, as only a gentleman would.

Two SophistiCATS
By Amy E. Zajac

In my job I traveled out of state five days a week. My two Coon cats, Bear and Bunny, part of my life long before I traveled, stayed home alone week after week. They enjoyed only each other's company during my absences.

They were born in the same litter at a friend's home in the California desert. As part of my family, they traveled around the country with me, as I moved from job to job during my career progression. All their needs satisfied, they always enjoyed plenty of food and water. I recently bought them an automatic kitty litter cleaning machine. I accommodated their physical comforts on every level, so I thought. But they lacked my attention four days a week and that created a pattern for my temperamental kitties.

When I arrived home every week, both Bear and Bunny welcomed me with their enthusiastic quiet patting. They stood on their hind quarters and patted smooth the fabric on the couch back upholstery with their declawed front paws, and waited for me to acknowledge them. They purred in their loudest voices and nudged my ankles, each competing for my attention. I patted and coddled them, as if I gave them confidence that I would stay around for awhile. Like clockwork, they both reversed focus, away from me, in their aristocratic and coon laid-back style of relaxed arrogance. They ignored my coddling and sweet words of greeting. Together, they jumped up onto the couch and snuggled into a single ball of fur.

After a few years, my parents moved in with me, which provided many mutual benefits, not the least of which, they took great care of my two temperamental friends. Bear and Bunny enjoyed this new daily attention from Mom and Dad, who talked to them, brushed their fur, and patted them regularly. I felt comfortable knowing all their needs were met. Yet they greeted me, week after week with the same warm enthusiasm that they showed me when they spent four days alone, followed by the abrupt reversal, ignoring me.

One Thursday I arrived home at my usual time. My Dad and I spoke for a few minutes. I took my suitcase downstairs. Everything appeared in order, just as I left it. One big difference — Bear and Bunny failed to greet me. I wondered why they hid from me. I missed the soft patting sound of Bear rubbing her paws on the back of the couch. Why isn't Bunny lying by the back door, mesmerized by birds or other animals close by? I looked around my living room, bedroom and bathroom. Out of the corner of my eye, I saw movement in a clothes basket among my clean clothes. Mom had brought them downstairs while I was away.

I knelt down next to the basket. "Oh there you are! Isn't this a cozy little spot you've found! No wonder you didn't welcome me. You probably knew I wouldn't approve of this, so you thought you'd hide out, didn't you?"

Bear and Bunny had burrowed into the center and cuddled up so closely together, they almost looked fused into one cat. Bear's head was nowhere to be seen. Bunny purred loudly as she nuzzled my hand. I saw Bear's sad black and gold eyes as she pulled her head out from under a shirt to welcome me home. Her long shaggy black tabby coat, totally in disarray, looked slept in when she stood up, arched her back, stretched, all a delay to say hello.

"There you are, Sweetie. I knew you'd come out, eventually. You know I'm going to have to wash everything over." Holding up a shirt to show to them, "Will you just look at all your black and gray hair on my favorite white blouse? You're probably thinking, *what's all the fuss about? If you leave the clothes out, you intended for us to have them as part of our domain. After all, you left us again for the week. Remember?*"

I thought about it and knew I'd need to let Mom know she can't leave any clothes baskets out in my main room. This way, my two sophisticated ladies, won't make the clothes basket into a new queen-sized bed ..As I talked to them they sat up and stared at me, as if they knew exactly what I said and readily accepted their cordial scolding. I think they expected it. After that, they turned and faced each other, licked each other's faces, and ignored my very existence.

Amazing Gracie

By John Leonard

Hungry and hurt, the scared little grey dog shivered. No one knew for sure how long she'd been running loose near the busy intersection in John's Creek, at least two weeks, according to those who tried to catch her. How had she had survived so long without being killed? Statistics estimate 10.000 cars pass through that one busy intersection every day, near the bank the dog called home. She managed to evade death this long, nothing short of a miracle, as she continued her insane game of dodging cars on the street. Somehow, she eluded death and her capture.

Some of her pursuers suggested the dog was feral. She showed no trust of human beings. One thought the creature was part wolf, coyote, or some other wild animal. Given her relatively small size and markings, a few people wondered if she could be a lost German Shepherd puppy. Guessing was close as anyone got. Even the most experienced dog handlers couldn't get near the dog.

The stray was injured; an angry red streak on her hind leg indicated she suffered from an ugly open wound. She needed medical attention, if someone could capture her.

The branch manager at the bank had enticed the dog to come near, using food and treats. Over a few days the dog developed a modicum of trust for the manager and made a hedge of shrubbery on the bank property her home base. Nevertheless, she shied away from human contact and foiled every effort to trap her. She accepted food from people, but nothing else.

The ranks of the volunteers trying to catch the evasive little dog swelled as others learned of her plight and wanted to save her from harm. But this dog was too smart and too quick. The group persisted, more desperate and determined than ever to succeed.

My wife and I were recruited by email, enthusiastic to join the hunt for the canine artful dodger. Lisa received a hot tip where the dog hid herself, on the bank grounds. Like police racing in response to an emergency, we sped off to the rescue, dog treats and rope leads in hand.

That morning Suzanne, another pursuer of the dog, went to the bank with a dual purpose. Suzanne had noticed the dog running loose on a previous visit and tried to catch her. She was determined and proved little more creative than the rest of us. Scrolling through her Rolodex, Suzanne contacted friends she knew would help. She was unaware that Lisa and I were already among the volunteers from the Forsyth County Humane Society (HSFC), organized and working to save the dog. Lisa was one of the ring leaders, a primary conspirator in the effort to catch the stray, so when Suzanne called, Lisa updated her. We had now improved our odds of success.

The dog remained hidden in the hedge less than ten feet from Suzanne as we arrived that morning. Suzanne knew that cats communicate peace with a slow blink. It's their own sign meant to put other felines at ease. She blinked slowly at the dog and she spoke gently to her. The sweet words turned into a calming lilt, and then into song. The dog apparently loved listening to her sing. Suzanne softly sang every song that came to mind, bringing some peace to the distrustful animal. She coaxed the animal almost within arm's reach. The dog stayed there for two hours in a cold steady drizzle.

Lisa parked our minivan. She slipped out the driver's door and pushed it closed with little noise, not to startle the stray. Lisa dropped to the ground and crawled toward Suzanne; I followed her example. When Lisa asked me if I could identify the dog's breed, I rose from my crouch and got a better look. I locked eyes on the dog's glare as she watched me. Her ears flattened out and flexed downward on the sides of her head like TV antennae adjusted for better reception. And then she disappeared into the evening gloom; a flash of grey sped away and disappeared into the night. Yes, I felt like a complete idiot. Suzanne just spent two hours in cold, damp, and miserable weather, working diligently to gain the dog's trust — and I ruined it in 30 seconds.

For the next several hours I walked around nearby businesses in the cold misting rain. I was miserable. I'd blown the best chance we had to bring this little stray to safety. In vain, I called out to the dog without a name. "Come here, baby. Sweetie, I won't hurt you. Here,, doggie." I searched under bushes, behind trashcans, and anywhere else I could think she might hide. She was long gone.

I remained distraught as we headed home, convinced someone would soon send out an email to announce that she'd been killed by a car. It would be my fault. The agony stayed with me for two weeks. I visualized streams of traffic passing through that intersection, never seeming to thin much, no matter the time of day. I would stop often and search the area, mindful that the clock ticked against the little grey dog's luck, and I feared it would soon run out.

One day I would fret when no new sightings of the dog were reported. The next day I marveled more time passed without receiving news of her death. Every day was a new ride on my roller coaster of emotions.

Two more weeks elapsed. People still sighted the dog running loose in the same vicinity. Those two weeks seemed an eternity. Then Lisa called me on my cell phone from her office. Breathless with excitement she told me someone caught the dog and wondered if I could go pick her up and take her to the vet. I grabbed my car keys and headed out the door as Lisa fed me the details on the run.

Lisa told me about another pursuer who had bought some turkey from a nearby deli and was able to hand-feed the stray. When the dog got close enough, the woman slipped a lead around the dog's neck. Apparently our canine fugitive had succumbed to hunger and seduced by the smell of Boar's Head Ovengold Turkey. My wife told me to hurry. The little dog panicked after being caught and the woman seriously considered letting her go, afraid she would hurt herself in the struggle to escape. The dog bucked and thrashed like a wild stallion, lassoed for the first time. Her captor became afraid to touch her.

When I arrived reinforcements had assembled for moral support, but *everyone* was afraid to touch this little grey dog. We had worked so hard to capture her, but now everyone acted as if she were a ravenous predator. I finally saw her clearly for the first time, a miniature German Shepherd Dog, perhaps a small Spitz, but with a straight tail instead of curled. The red wound on her hind leg looked ugly, but she was a beautiful little girl.

Though forewarned by everyone, I was determined not to fail this animal a second time. When I looked at her, I saw an exhausted and frightened little dog, not a beast to be feared. I slowed to a more casual pace as I approached and looked for any signs of aggression. Her ears flattened again in the same unhappy position I'd seen before. She wanted to run, not bite me. I gently scooped her into my arms and carried her to our van, laying her in the kennel we'd kept in the back for the last two weeks. I gripped the rope lead in my hand, in case she managed to wriggle free.

Now, I wanted to calm and comfort the frightened little dog as much as possible. Speaking words in a soft voice seemed the right thing. In the 20 minute drive to the vet's office, I listened to her whine about her captivity. Preventing a rough ride, I took it slow, using my most soothing voice to comfort her, but it didn't seem to help. A memory. Suzanne sang to this dog on that cold rainy day, and it *soothed the savage beast*, as the expression goes. Desperate times call for desperate measures. Although I can't carry a tune in a bucket, I sang every song I could remember during those 20 minutes to the vet. Lullabies, hymns, popular tunes, any song I knew words to and made up new lyrics. Our granddaughter Ava Grace loves to hear me sing, "You Are My Sunshine." I knew a verse or two, so I tried it out on the little grey dog. For some reason she quieted, so I crooned the verses over and over on the last leg of our journey.

When I reached the vet and opened the kennel door, I was pleased the dog didn't make a mad dash for freedom. She seemed much calmer than she'd been at the bank. I carried her in my arms into an examination room. The veterinarian examined her and decided she was a Norwegian Elkhound mix. He needed to sedate her to examine her leg, so he suggested he keep her overnight.

The next morning the vet technician brought the grey dog back to me. She looked at me warily, like she couldn't quite remember me. I spoke to her in the same voice I used to soothe and comfort her the day before. Her whole body quivered with joy — and not just her tail.

I admit it. I fell in love. *How do I break the news to my wife?* By this time, she wasn't threatened by four-legged competition. The vet determined her injury healed enough on its own, so he recommended an antibiotic ointment to help it heal fully. She was ready for the next step, inoculations prior to adoption. That meant she needed to be quarantined for at least ten days to prevent spreading disease at the shelter. Of course, no other quarantine option came to mind, except my house. I was perfectly happy to add her to the pack, even if it was only temporary. The dog appeared reluctant to bond with anyone but my wife and me.

Once she entered the HSFC adoption program, the little grey hound needed a means of identification for tracking purposes. She became D5017, the D for dog, and 5016 dogs preceded her in the program. Lisa and I agreed we would foster

D5017 until she was adopted or she went to the shelter. Of course, I had other ideas in mind for the length of her stay.

Because we have several large dogs as both permanent and foster residents of our home, we segregated our new addition from the pack and planned to introduce them gradually. To get her more accustomed to human contact, I slept with her on the floor of the guest bedroom the first few nights. That strange behavior merited the arching of Lisa's eyebrows. Gradually we mixed her in with the pack, first with the established permanent pack, followed by the less stable members, our foster dogs. After D5017 met everyone, we all went for a walk together.

Calling our first effort a walk is a stretch of the imagination, especially because I carried the new dog most of the way. I put her on the ground to encourage her do her business, but she was so nervous, she chose not to. A whole day passed, and her biological dam burst. It had gotten to the point that I was ready to call the vet, fearing a bowel obstruction or some other serious medical issue.

We named D5017 Gracie, after our granddaughter Ava Grace. They both liked to hear me sing, "You Are My Sunshine." I had worried that Gracie might act inappropriately around the pack. She was so small; I feared she could get hurt. But Gracie proved much more comfortable in the company of other dogs than the company of people.

Briefly we kept Gracie separated from the pack by a wooden child security gate, but she chewed it into splinters in short order. The floor looked littered with a thousand toothpicks.

Lisa has said that we only keep the dogs that are so broken, they don't fit anywhere else. I have a slightly different perspective. I think some dogs like Gracie are a bit smarter than others. Unlike our other permanent pack members, Gracie didn't display any pseudo-behavioral problems that only appeared in other homes and disappeared in ours. We also knew she wasn't normal from the first day we had her. So, she belonged in our home. Shortly after we started fostering her, we formally adopted Gracie from the HSFC.

We knew Gracie needed us and we needed her. We weren't sure at first Gracie felt the same way about her new family. The acid test came. At a nearby park, when I bent to tie my shoe, somehow Gracie pulled her leash out from my grasp. Lisa gave chase, but like a child playing tag, it seemed like fun to Gracie. The harder Lisa chased, the wider the gap grew between them. Gracie ran only so Lisa would chase her. Of course, my wife had no hope of catching her. Eventually she realized this and stopped trying. She positioned herself between Gracie and the park exit, which led out to a dangerous highway. Lisa looked like a hapless linebacker, struggling to fill a huge gap in the line. Gracie played the elite running back, about to shake off her last potential tackler before gaining an unobstructed open field.

I gave up tying my shoelace. I knew I couldn't catch Gracie, with or without my laces tied. More than thirty yards separated us, and she was fast. If I chased her, she would just run in the opposite direction.

I remained kneeled and used my special voice to call her. It was a huge gamble. The stakes were high. Gracie was seconds away from a clean escape. No telling where she would roam. We were far from her old stomping grounds. I could see her waver between the lure of the great unknown and the siren call of my special voice. She made her decision. Gracie ran toward me at breakneck speed. As she drew near, she gave no indication she planned to stop once she reached me. It felt like this might be one last drive-by taunt before she left us for good.

Responsible for losing her once, I wasn't willing to risk it. *This could be my only chance.* I rationalized, told myself, from my kneeling position, it wouldn't hurt much when I dove face-first toward the asphalt as I grabbed for the leash when Gracie passed by.

I lied. As I grasped the leash, it hurt far more than I expected, but not as much as letting her get away.

* * * *

Gracie has been with us for several years. I trust her not to run away. Sometimes she looks wild-eyed, as if she doesn't recognize me. To be on the safe side, over the years we have fattened her up just enough to make sure she's a little easier to catch, in case she does try to run off again.

In fact, Lisa has a new nickname for Gracie. She calls her "my little butterball." Just for the record, her whole body still shakes with joy when I sing "You Are My Sunshine." And she's still a sucker for Boar's Head Ovengold Turkey.

Hot Dogs & Cool Cats

Trauma Tale Entrees

Birds in My Bra
By Donna Sundblad

    I peeked inside the twelve-by-twelve plywood nest box. Sparkle, one of my gray cockatiels, warmed her first clutch of three eggs. Her mate Radar sat in the corner like a father waiting in a hospital room for the news. I'd raised Radar from a baby. Now he would be a daddy.

    Cockatiels birth offspring in gray, yellow, or cinnamon, or with interesting variegations. Birds with rare or unique coloration cost more money. Both Sparkle and Radar belonged to the common type known as *normal gray*, but with their genetics, they could produce much more coveted yellow babies. Sparkle's common coloring had a little extra flare; tiny flecks of yellow sprinkled her powder-gray breast, reminding me of a Fourth of July sparkler. That's where she got her name.

    "It's close," I told my husband. "I think Radar is sitting on two of the eggs. The other one is about to hatch."

During the brooding process, Radar sat on the eggs during the day, and Sparkle kept them warm at night. All seemed normal. Being their first clutch, I wondered if they'd know what to do. While I raised Radar from a baby, Sparkle's history remained a mystery. Friends had called me, thinking one of my birds had gotten out. Well, as a result, Sparkle joined our flock.

I walked to the kitchen to clean up after dinner. The cage and nest box sat about ten paces away in the family room. I turned off the water at the tap and heard it, a faint rhythmic peep. "I hear a baby!" I hurried to the nest box, slid the hatch up, and peeked inside. Sparkle hovered over her one egg blocking my view, but off to the side I spotted a telltale half eggshell on the wood shavings between the birds. I wanted just a peek. Would the baby be a normal gray or a pretty yellow? Every hatchling wears a downy yellow coat which they lose as their feathers come in, but the color of the eyes, even before they can see, would tell me. Red eyes meant a yellow bird, dark eyes; the baby would be a normal gray. Finding homes for a more coveted yellow bird would prove easy.

I slipped my fingertips into the box. Sparkle lunged at my hand, a cockatiel intimidation technique, a mother protecting her young. A tiny pink bird, an inch long and covered in matted yellow down, struggled to hold its head up without success. It rolled onto its back, its clumsy feet in the air. Something didn't look right. I thrust my hand in and scooped the baby into my palm before the parents reacted. The bloody tip of its rear toe alarmed me. "What happened to your toe, baby bird?" A tiny bit of blood oozed from a missing toenail on its back toe. *What do I do? One of the parents must have bitten it off!*

Normally I let the parents feed their chicks for two weeks, until they got bigger. Then I would pull them from the nest and hand-feed them for another month to six weeks. Handfed baby cockatiels made great pets. I closed my hand around the tiny life. *They must have thought the toenail didn't belong. Curious.* I slipped the little critter back in place, next to the two remaining eggs. Radar took over the care of his new baby. I'd check the toe again in a little while; just to be sure it was okay.

The sound of the quick-paced peep-peep-peep signaled the parents feeding the baby. *That's a good sign.* When the chirping stopped, I walked over and peered into the box. I used a tap-my-finger diversion to get Radar to move. The little bird rolled onto its back with feet in the air. Instead of back toes, the bird had little bloody stumps. My mind raced. *What have they done? How will this bird perch without back toes?* I pulled the baby from the box and clutched it in my hand. *What am I going to do? I can't risk putting it back in there.*

I went to the refrigerator with the baby bird nestled in my palm. With my free hand, I shuffled items on the top shelf. I pulled the canister of baby bird formula from the back and shook it. *Plenty. A bird this size certainly won't eat much.* The helpless bird squirmed against my palm. It scared me. *How will I feed such a tiny life?*

The baby had just eaten, so it would be okay for a couple of hours. I mentally prepared to get up every two hours throughout the night and check to see if it needed to be fed. That wasn't the immediate problem. *How will I keep it warm?* In the past, when I pulled babies from the nest at two weeks, they were old enough that they knew to huddle together for warmth. *A heating pad will be too hot, unless....*

I went to the garage, carried an aquarium I used to raise baby birds, and set it up with a towel and heating pad below it, dialed to low, a makeshift brooder. And I prayed. My first check on the baby during the night ensured me all was well. The second time I awoke, I fed it a few drops of baby bird formula. *If this bird lives, it will be a miracle. But what will it do without back toes? And what about the other eggs?* Too tired to think about it, I shuffled back to bed.

The following morning the baby ate heartily. I breathed easier. I had the next two days off from work. As I fed my other six cockatiels, I accepted the new baby as part of my flock; without its toes, I wouldn't find it a home.

When I heard the chirp of a second chick two days later, I rushed to the nest box. Sure enough blood seeped from the tip of one toe. I pulled it, immediately. Feeding two babies wouldn't really be any more work than one, but what would I do with them when I had to go to work the next day? My current duties required me to be out of the office for the next few days, while I took inventory in vacation rental properties along the beach.

Thoughts of what to do with the babies consumed me. During one of the night feedings, I came up with a plan. The following day, I lined the center of my bra with paper towel and placed the two babies into their makeshift nest next to my skin for warmth. I checked in the mirror to make sure I didn't look like a triple-breasted mother bird, and headed out the door. It worked perfectly, though the squirming against my chest took some getting used to. I stopped, fed them on schedule, and performed inventory. Checking bottom cabinets to count pots and pans, I made sure I stooped without bending too far forward; I didn't want the birds to tumble into my shirt.

Over the three days of inventory, the baby cockatiels grew stronger and peeped often. The third egg didn't hatch. I sent Radar and Sparkle back into the cage with my other cockatiels — they would not be having any more children.

The following day I returned to desk duty in the office. I followed the same plan. Just one thing; I hadn't considered their squeaky *peep, peep, peep* that I had grown so accustomed to. The sounds were barely audible. I didn't think anyone would notice. As I stood at the front desk and discussed a work order with Margie, little squeaks escaped from my chest. Margie stopped taking notes and looked around. "What's that noise?"

My face heated with embarrassment. *How on earth am I going to explain this?* "Can you keep a secret?" I reached in the neck of my shirt and pulled a baby bird from my bra. She stared at it wide-eyed as I told her the story. We laughed about it throughout the day, but she failed restraint, and asked me several time to, "Show them those babies." Some secret! The following day I carried the aquarium to and from the office.

The babies ate about every four hours, so I used my breaks and lunch time to feed them. Customers and vendors stopped by the office to see the birds. Their pin feathers grew in. The older of the two became affectionately known as Cripple Bird. She could stand, but she had a hard time climbing the ladder I placed in the aquarium to help them learn to perch.

To my surprise, as the babies weaned at six weeks, Cripple Bird found a new home and a new name. One of the women who cleaned the rental properties adopted her. That left her sister, who, unfortunately, lacked a friendly personality. As a gray female, she lacked both the bright yellow face and the ability to talk that made her male counterparts more desirable to those who wanted a "pretty" bird or a pet that could talk. The young bird wasn't mean, but she made it clear she wanted to be left alone. With her less-than-friendly disposition, she joined my flock for years. I named her Tweetpie, an effort to erase her negative reputation. Even with part of her back toe missing, she dominated the cage and bossed the other six cockatiels around, including her parents. I handled her often, in an effort to make her friendly, and she tolerated me. In our own way we grew close.

When circumstances brought my daughter and her family to live with us, my grandchildren loved all the birds. My granddaughter Taylor's favorite was Tweetpie. "The silver bird is the prettiest bird." *Silver bird.* The pseudonym brought a smile to my face. Taylor held Tweetpie regularly, and the persnickety bird grew to enjoy sitting on Taylor's shoulder. To my amazement, every once in a while Tweetpie tipped her head to be scratched; a *friendly* cockatiel gesture!

I continued raising baby birds with a different breeding pair. A family friend with four children, shopping for a pet, chose a male cinnamon cockatiel—because they wanted a bird that would learn to talk. He didn't let them down. Melody learned to whistle, talk, and became the star of their household. When visiting our home, the mother of the family always stopped by the cage and admired Tweetpie. "She's the prettiest bird."

When their first bird, Melody, reached one-year old, the family decided they wanted another cockatiel to keep their cinnamon company. "I won't have babies for at least a couple of months," I said.

"I'd like one that looks like Tweetpie," the mother said.

"You could have her." I knew I had to be honest. "She's four-years-old and set in her habits." I told her our history together, about her rocky start, that her personality was less than friendly.

"Really? You'd let me have her?" Expectation glistened in her blue eyes.

I couldn't believe it. She knew the bird's faults and wanted her! The woman held Tweetpie as if she were precious, like silver, and loved her missing toe, crotchety disposition, everything. Today Tweetpie lives with her companion bird and a loving family. Thinking back to her difficult start, I never thought it possible. When I visit their home, Tweepie is always happy to see me. Looking past her growing-up years, I admire the beauty she has become with a special fondness.

Sasha

By Amy E. Zajac

    While visiting my daughter in Washington, I received a telephone call from my parents who shared my Georgia home with me. A lost dog wandered onto our property after I left on vacation. They wanted to know if I thought a new dog would be good for our family. I immediately rejected the idea. "Our family owns enough pets." At the time we owned a dog and five cats.

    My firm statement didn't stop their pushing for the new dog. "She is so different, a Siberian Husky with beautiful light blue eyes, and a gentle and understanding manner. You'll just love her!"

I held my ground, "We don't need another pet. Not only don't we have the space, but we'd need to make yet another financial commitment for all her medical needs and for feeding this dog nourishing quality meals."

Even though my parents were sad, they backed off. At the same time they took to this dog, so did my sister and her husband who lived next door. They waited to hear if the former owner would come and claim her. They didn't. My sister eventually kept the dog.

They named her Sasha and she adapted quickly to my sister's family life. A few weeks passed, and we all found out Sasha would soon deliver a litter of pups. With no garage at my sister's house, my garage became Sasha's delivery room … birthing ten puppies. After she and all of us survived this, I saw Sasha transform into an amazingly loving mother. She endured the separation from each of her children as homes were found for them all.

Although Sasha proved to be a great house dog, my sister's family kept her outside. She figured Sasha lived outside as her lifestyle prior to her arrival. So Sasha shared time with us, endearing herself to my house, especially to my parents. We enjoyed her daily visits and developed personal relationships with her, as she spent hours with us in our house every day. Sasha charmed us by her love and devotion.

My sister and her husband pressed us to keep Sasha outside during the day while they were at work instead of inside our house. Her sweet personality tugged at our heartstrings when she arrived at our door. Her pleading eyes softened our resolve to abide by my sister's request, and once again we let her inside. Once more, my sister pleaded her case, and we decided to follow through for her. The next time Sasha showed up at our door, we refused her entry. She sat on our porch most of that day and every day for weeks.

After a while Sasha didn't show up on a regular basis. She developed other patterns for her daily life while my sister and her husband worked. We adjusted to Sasha's absence. She showed up at my sister's house every evening for her food and camaraderie with my sister's family.

About midway through one afternoon, Sasha crept into our garage without my dad hearing her. She lay behind him while he worked at repairing something on his bench. When dad stood up to take a break, he saw Sasha. "Hey there, girl, when did you get here?" She didn't react as usual. Dad bent over to pat her. She whimpered and didn't move. "Can you get up? Come here, Sasha Girl." Sasha remained still. He yelled for my mother to come out to the garage; as she tried to move Sasha, the dog whined, whimpered, and barked. They guessed Sasha was in pain.

My parents, when they managed to get her into their car, drove her to our veterinarian. The vet determined Sasha's pelvis was broken. "Sasha was hit by a vehicle. I've seen injuries like this before."

The doctor scratched her head. "Why did you bring her in? I thought the dog belonged to your daughter." My parents explained how Sasha showed up in our garage. "Oh, I see. You know, she struggled to return where she believed was her home. I know it's true. Despite her terrible pain, she dragged herself into *your* garage."

After my parents told me what the vet said, I called my sister. "I want Sasha." I abandoned the ridiculous notion that we didn't need any more pets and couldn't afford to keep her. In her pain she came to the place where she knew was home, where she'd be cared for.

We are rewarded day after day by Sasha's loyalty and friendship from the day she crawled back to our garage ... and into my heart.

Happily, I can report, after eight weeks of very copious attention by my mother, Sasha returned to perfect health, with no tell-tale signs of the broken pelvis.

Teri and the Cat
By Béla M. Krusac

    The thin, hungry tortoise shell cat crouched low in the underbrush of the woods at the edge of the clearing. Her eyes followed the human being's every move. Teri spotted the cat peripherally as she scrubbed the RV with a large sponge. She'd noticed the stray stalking the home over the last few days and suspected it was hungry. Without looking directly at it, she slowly set the sponge into the bucket and dried her hands.

    The cat watched as the gray haired woman spooned food from a can onto a white saucer. The wind wafted the smell toward the woods; the stray focused on the prize. As the woman disappeared into the RV, it rose without moving a whisker, moved her big green eyes from side to side, and waited. The cat lunged forward just a step, hesitated as if she were considering her actions, and twitched her shoulders. In a flash it darted for the food, maybe the first real meal in days.

    Teri watched the cat through the slits of the blinds as it devoured the tasty brown morsels and licked the saucer to a dishwasher-clean sparkle. She opened the door of the RV with painstaking care not to make noise. The sated cat sat in silence and licked its chops. But one old hinge on the metal door squeaked, a shockwave telegraph to a stray. She streaked for the underbrush of the nearby woods and disappeared.

    For the next three days food was left out, closer and closer to the front door of the Thomas home. On the fourth day, the cat waited at the front door for its meal. From that day on, Teri and the cat bonded inseparable. She called the cat Kizia. Where one was, the other was not far away.

Teri and her husband Max took the RV on excursions, escape mini-vacations, whenever the timing worked out. One hot summer, a few years later, the winds of adventure stirred Teri's soul, and they went on a five day trip down the Natchez Trail, leaving Kizia with my wife, Christy to cat sit. Kizia lay in the shade of the porch and waited for her mistress to love and feed her, but Teri didn't come. She barely touched the food and water in the bowl, and Christy suspected Kizia was lonely and depressed.

On the third morning, my turn to feed her, Kizia was gone. Our hearts sank as we knew how much love and affection Teri had for this cat. We searched everywhere, knowing the Thomas motor home would return in less than two days.

"Kizia, where are you?" Christy called out. I felt the fear in her voice. She was left in charge of her mother's beloved pet. Now the cat ran off. Did she become another tragic road kill? As beautiful a cat as she was, did someone pick her up from our yard? Agonizing questions swirled through our minds as we searched everywhere we could think of where a cat might hide. Kizia was gone. Our family vehicle, in the shop for repairs, exacerbated the search, so we both looked for Kizia on foot.

"Why don't you go down the road," Christy asked me, "and knock on doors. See if anyone has seen her?"

"It's over ninety degrees, not even noon!" I wiped a bead of sweat from my forehead. The thought of hiking up the steep hill that led away from our home....in search of a stray cat ... well, it wasn't a cherished thought. Neither was how I'd greet my mother-in-law with the loss of her Kizia, I started my hike up the road. Our neighbors were kind and sympathetic, but no one had seen Kizia. I walked an hour in one direction in blistering heat, now felt the pavement burn beneath my tennis shoes. Stepping off the blacktop, I trod along the gravel strip beside the road.

You idiot! Why didn't you bring some water? I now had the experience, understanding the meaning of the phrase *cotton mouth*. I stopped to rest, As I decided to turn around and end this search, I noticed a small home set back in the woods. Water! They have water, and shade! Cool shade! I wanted out of the sun, and more than that, a drink.

With a quickened pace I headed for the cool shadows of the cottonwood trees. Four stairs led up to a screened-in porch of the old cottage. I opened the squeaky screen door. Kizia lay right there, in the shade of the porch beside a half empty bowl of water. I knocked on the door, introduced myself to the lady of the house, and explained our predicament.

The lady said Kizia wandered up to her porch a few hours ago, looking very thirsty and tired. So she took her in. "You look rather thirsty, yourself. Can I get you a drink?"

"Please. My lips are so dry, it hurts to talk."

She disappeared behind the screen door to bring me a drink. I stroked Kizia's fur with the satisfaction of a victorious hunter. The screen door opened, my hand wrapped around a cold, sweaty glass, and the liquid of life bathed my tongue in glory. I drank every drop.

"Can I get you more?"

"Oh, no," I didn't want to put her out again, but I really wanted another. We exchanged pleasantries. I picked up Kizia, pushed open the squeaky porch door, and headed down the shaded path that led to the blistering hot pavement.

I hadn't taken but a few steps down the path, when I realized I had gone up and down the steep hill … and had it to face the journey in reverse, this time carrying a feisty cat. I stepped back onto the road. I could see the heat essence rise from the black-tarred surface; mirage puddles shimmered in the distance. I started back up the agonizing hill.

As we neared the crest, Kizia freed a leg and scratched my bare arm, drawing blood. She leaped into the brambles alongside the road. The thicket held her for a moment. I grabbed her with a predatory lunge, leaving streaks of my own flesh on the thorny vines. I locked her front paws in a death grip and mumbled words of displeasure into her ears. She meowed back, as if she felt the same way about me, but remained passive. I realized now that I would never make it home if I had to carry Kizia like this. It was either her or me, and I decided in favor of me. Furious, I cocked my arms, aiming to toss this nasty cat into the brambles. An SUV pulled up. It was my former neighbor, Donna.

"Looks like you've got your hands full. Want a ride?"

"You are an angel!" I climbed into the vehicle and tossed the cat into the back without asking.

"Looks like kitty got the better of you." Donna stared at the bloody scratches running down my arms and legs.

"Yeah, but I rescued her." My teeth remained clenched.

We secured the cat in the garage, gave her food and water, and I went home for a long, cold bath. As I drifted to sleep, despite the sting from claws and thorns down my arms and legs, I felt like a hero. I saved Christy the embarrassment of having to tell Teri she lost her cat. I saved Teri from the heartache of losing her love. And I did save Kizia from a life of loneliness, separated from her loving family. The world was set right again.

Spitfire

By John Leonard

"There's a kitten in foster care that can't go to the shelter," my wife Lisa said. "The foster mom can't keep her anymore, because her landlord complained. Where can she go?"

Whenever there was "no place else for an animal to go," our house became the critter refuge of last resort. I wondered how many animals have had their lives depend upon the availability of our house. Yes, we received joy in saving lives, though I often grumbled about the perpetual revolving door of animals — I secretly enjoyed having them. Most of them.

And then we fostered Spitfire. Before bringing home this diminutive flea-ridden bundle of attitude, Lisa forewarned me, the kitten is disabled. She is missing her right front leg.

We put her in the safety of the guest bedroom and let her out of the carrier. The kitten burst out of her cage in full attack mode, crazed by her incarceration. She bit and scratched us, anything she could to deny our offered affection.

Then there were the fleas. I suggested we bathe her. Lisa's exasperation reflected on her face, conveying in detail what she thought of the idea. My wife applied a dry powered flea treatment on the cat, and, within a few days, the problem was solved.

Next project, naming the cat. I suggested Tripod, a play on her physical condition. Lisa ignored me. After a few days, Lisa again mentioned the cat's lack of a name. She explained that she couldn't market the kitten online without a name. I repeated my suggestion of a name for her, Tripod.

"Sweetheart, how many three-legged dogs or cats have you known in your life?" I read condescension in her voice, the best patience she could come up with.

"Three or four, I guess."

"How many of them were called Tripod?"

I didn't like the rejection, but Lisa has never been a big fan of puns. The kitten went without a name a while longer. I began calling her Fleabag, even though I knew she was cured. Lisa suggested that the kitten's personality should dictate the selection of her name. I worked on that. Handicapped would be a poor choice of words for advertising, but Overcompensating seemed much more appropriate. Vicious worked, too.

The little fur ball proved not to have an affectionate bone in her body, especially when we retired for the night. She hunched and arched her back like a witch's black cat, except she was orange calico. Without much warning, she'd would spring into the air and pounce on an unsuspecting foot moving under the covers — while the person attached to the foot was fast asleep. Because she lacked two front paws with which to trap her prey, the kitten used her needle sharp teeth more frequently than normal cats. Every member of our household soon bore tiny scars to remind them of our little Spitfire. Lisa probably came up with the name first, but, in reality, the kitten named herself, Spitfire.

Not completely anti-social, Spitfire liked to play, but it always felt more like she toyed with prey intending to kill and eat it. As soon as she got bored, someone paid the price.

Carrying this cat was no fun. My forearms got covered with superficial bite and scratch marks. I received deeper scratches on my chest and stomach, where she used her hind legs as a springboard, escaping from any affection I wanted to show her.

She gave us a scare one day. I had a toy similar to a pompom, with a long tassel of plastic streamers. Spitfire loved to attack it. We played for a while. I laughed when I saw how winded she'd become; Spitfire panted like a dog. I didn't know that cats aren't supposed to pant like dogs — it's a sign of respiratory distress. She began to convulse as I put her back into her room. I yelled, "Lisa! The kitten is having a seizure!"

Lisa raced upstairs, grabbed the kitten, wrapped her in a towel, and forced her finger into Spitfire's mouth, she said, to keep her from biting her tongue. I ran for the cell phone and punched in the vet's number. By that time Spitfire threw up a piece of a streamer that she'd swallowed. I threw the rest of the toy into the trash. We chose safer objects for play, like the *kitten mitten*, a glove with long wire fingers, with which we wrestled with Spitfire from a safe distance.

I realized she would soon lose her kitten cuteness and become hard to find her "forever" home. The longer we procrastinated, rehabilitating her bad behavior, the longer it would take to place her. We weren't doing Spitfire any favors, allowing her anti-social behavior to continue. But Spitfire liked to be around people. I suspected, proximity made it easier for her to inflict pain, but affection remained a foreign concept. Lisa expressed concerns when our allergies worsened, a big reason why we don't have cats living in our home for very long. And Lisa feared that Spitfire was not adoptable. I thought up a strategy to communicate affection to the kitten.

I brought Spitfire into our bedroom several times each day, but, instead of releasing her to play, I held her until she would permit affection. If she struggled and resisted, I took her back to her bedroom, left her for a few minutes, and tried again. I was determined to train the kitten enough so that she would allow me to pet her.

It only took a few days before Spitfire got the message. If she wanted to be around people, she had to allow human affection in return for the reward of play. She quickly learned to keep her claws retracted and to *mouth* her humans gently, instead of biting them hard enough to draw blood. Spitfire still bit and scratched us, because that was her way to tell us she wanted back in her room. While I trained her, she trained me.

The day finally came when Lisa took Spitfire to the shelter. She had grown and it was time, however sad to say goodbye. Soon her future parents would find the kitten and take her to her forever home. Our scars have all healed, and we knew she never intended to hurt anyone. Nevertheless, our hearts took on some pain … when we parted with our little Spitfire.

Lucky

By Donna Sundblad

    A motley group of teenage boys stood in small clusters in the empty lots behind the houses lining the east side of Grove Avenue. "There it is. Over there," one of the boys said. He pointed toward a pile of debris hidden by weeds and tall grass. A dog's bark with a protective edge chopped the air in staccato bursts. The only girl, I stood to the side and scanned the open area, looking for the source. A flash of dark fur near the debris pile caught my attention and blended into the late summer foliage.

    "She's got puppies in there," Tom said. He walked to the pile of old boards and miscellaneous junk and teased the dog, trying to lure her from her hiding place.

    Eleven-year-old Steve, the youngest of the bunch, said, "Poke a stick in there. Maybe that will get her to come out."

    I stood in silence, hoping to get a glimpse of the puppies. The boys finally tricked the mother into leaving her lair beneath the rubble. Once she was in the open, we caught a peek of the puppies, Brown, black, and bits of white, a litter about six to eight weeks old. The mother did her best to protect her babies from the intruders, but her babies were soon disbursed among the neighborhood children. The mother dog returned to an empty nest.

    I counted myself among the fortunate. The black puppy I carried home had short hair, a pointed nose, and a curly tail. In my way of thinking, he was lucky to have escaped the dogcatcher. Before I stepped foot into the house, I knew his name was Lucky.

    Talking my parents into keeping the puppy took only two days. I knew they couldn't help but fall in love with his floppy ears and dark brown eyes. His puppy charm melted their excuses for why we couldn't have a dog.

Steve owned one of Lucky's brothers and lived next door. He decided to have an overnighter with the other boys and their new puppies, but, because I was the only female dog owner, I wasn't invited. The boys camped out in the garage with their dogs, having a good time, until the next morning when the mother dog showed up. She prowled outside the garage, looking for a way to get to her babies. Mother Dog must have been able to smell her puppies all gathered in one place.

The boys chased her off with stones, and she ended up on our front porch. I peeked out at the dog, cowering in the corner where two brick walls came together. I looked over at Lucky. "Come here, Lucky." I patted my leg. He crossed the floor in clumsy puppy fashion, wagging his curly tail. I picked him up, and he planted wet kisses all over my face. The thought of what I was about to do scared me. I took a deep breath and opened the door, holding the squirming puppy in my arms.

Mother Dog looked up at me with wary brown eyes, but then she saw her pup. She stood, giving me a clear view of her swollen teats. I felt awful for her as I inched the screen door opened, Lucky in one hand, and squeezed onto the porch. The door clicked closed behind me. "It's okay," I said. I used as calm a voice as possible. Dropping to my knees, I put Lucky on the cement across from his mother. His little tail wagged furiously as they sniffed each other. The reunion brought tears to my eyes.

"Lucky," I called, hoping he would return to me. The little black ball of fur turned his head and looked at me with those deep brown eyes. "Come on, Lucky." I patted the cement. He ambled back to me on his lanky puppy legs. What a relief! But my joy was cut short. The fur on Mother Dog's neck stood on end. I put my puppy back onto the porch floor, ever so slowly. Lucky ran back to his mother. This cycle repeated; Lucky traveled back and forth.

Finally, I lifted Lucky into my arms and talked to Mother Dog. "Do you want your puppy?" I asked as if she would answer. She was not an attractive dog. A long broad body on short legs, but she was a good mother. I approached her cautiously with her puppy, my puppy, as a peace offering. I placed Lucky next to her. She didn't recoil or growl. I released Lucky and rested my hand on his back. Mother Dog sniffed my hand. Much to my relief, she found me acceptable. I looked into her eyes, reached over, and petted her head. Her thick tail thudded against the cement, sweeping dust aside like a broom.

The menacing older dog transformed. First, she sniffed my fingers. Her brown eyes checked me out. I wasn't sure what to think, until she licked my hand. How rewarding it was for me to build that trust. I wondered about her previous owners — she must have had an owner, because she accepted human contact rather easily. I walked into the house and let Mom know, leaving Lucky with his mother. Mom stepped onto the porch with me. Lucky tried to rough and tumble with his mom, but she lay, patiently enduring rather than joining in. I knelt beside her again and stroked her dark brown coat. She needed a bath. "Can we keep her, Mom?"

"Donna, we can't have two dogs." My heart fell. Mom put her hand on my shoulder. Tears blurred my vision and dropped from my cheeks onto the cement. "Donna, you'd have a zoo, if we would allow it. We can't afford it."

She was right.

"We will have to find a home for her or call the animal shelter."

No one wanted the older dog ... except me. We called the animal shelter, and they came to collect her. I watched them take her away and struggled with guilt. I had betrayed her. Perhaps she would have been better off if I hadn't taught her to trust. I hugged my puppy and vowed I would care for him and love him all his life.

He remained our family dog for sixteen years. His loyalty and companionship brought years of enjoyment, but I often contemplate the unknown fate of the stray dog that gave him birth. It was a life lesson for me. I learned the importance of not taking on the responsibility of a pet, if you're not ready to see that commitment through to the end … because the one who pays the price is the pet that trusts you.

A Real Trooper
By John Leonard

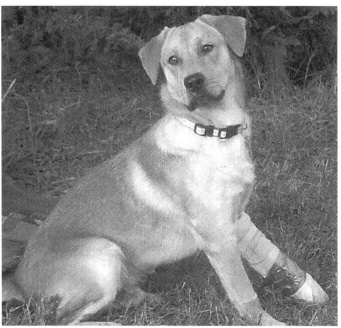

If cats have nine lives, how many does a dog have?
Decisions of life and death take their toll on me. It's not easy to be president of the Humane Society of Forsyth County.

I recognized her phone number on the call display. "Lisa, thank God you answered your phone."

"Hi, Leslie. What's the matter?"

"I just found a dog that was hit by a car lying on the side of the road. I thought he might already be dead. I only stopped and got out to make sure there was nothing I could do. I really can't believe he's still alive. The poor thing ... his legs were all twisted and his body is scraped and bloody. Even the skin on his nose is rubbed off. The worst is his head injury. It breaks my heart to see how badly he's hurt – at first I was sure he was dead. But as I turned back toward my car, I saw his chest move."

Leslie finally paused to take a breath before plowing forward. "Lisa, he evacuated his bowels. I had some rags in my trunk and cleaned him up as best I could ... but he's dying. Please, can the Humane Society help him? I don't know where else to take him or what to do."

Her torrent of words hit me like a hammer. Another good-hearted volunteer with yet another crisis. How could I say no?

We operate a small, no-kill rescue shelter. Most of our volunteers will stop to help a live dog running loose on the road, but who stops for a dead dog?

My guess is only the ones who have hearts of gold.

Leslie sounded calm, but her voice cracked with emotion. We both knew bowel evacuation usually portended death.

I asked Leslie a couple of questions to help me decide which vet would be closest.

"Yes, Leslie. We'll try to help the dog. Do you know Dr. McGruder at Crestview Animal Hospital? His clinic is closest to you, and they'll take really good care of him. I'll call ahead to let them know you're on your way."

I prayed the dog would live long enough to reach Crestview.

Our Humane Society is a non-profit organization with limited resources. Our sole purpose is to save lives, but which ones?

If his injuries are too severe for the dog to recover enough to enjoy life, the humane thing will be to euthanize him. Dr. McGruder is well aware of our limited budget and supports what we do. He'll give me good advice; know the right thing to do. I can't stand the idea of any animal suffering needlessly.

I took a deep breath and made the call.

Leslie arrived at the clinic with the dog while I was still on the phone. The receptionist offered to call me back after he had been evaluated.

Within an hour, the receptionist called me back as promised. After we spoke briefly, she put me on hold.

Dr. McGruder came on the line. He seems cantankerous to some people, but I know under his gruff exterior beats a heart of gold.

"His current condition is extremely critical, but stable. We've given him pain medication and we'll be monitoring his condition closely. I had to splint his front paw. It's too early to tell the extent of any brain damage. He can't be sedated to operate on the leg because of the risk of permanent damage from the injury to his brain. I'm worried about swelling. We'll keep him comfortable and monitor his progress. I'll call you tomorrow and give you an update."

The dog survived transport to the veterinary hospital. We assigned him a number and entered him into our database as an official Humane Society dog. He became D5747 for tracking purposes. Dogs don't respond to names like D5747. Because no one knew anything about the dog prior to Leslie finding him, I named him Trooper for his perseverance and will to live.

Trooper survived his first night at Crestview.

The following morning Dr. McGruder called as promised. "He's still alive, but he can't sit up, eat or control his head."

My stomach knotted. *Dr. McGruder doesn't mince words. He's painting a grim picture.*

Anticipating the worst, I asked: "What's your recommendation?"

"It's still a little too early to tell. Basically, we're just boarding and monitoring the dog to make sure he doesn't suffer needless pain. I'm giving him intravenous pain meds in the fluids we're giving to keep him hydrated. He doesn't seem to be able to drink water yet. It's not expensive to board him. We can continue to treat his symptoms. Let's give it time and see."

Silently, I breathed a sigh of relief. I was pulling for him, but experience with reality told me not to let my hopes get too high.

And I wasn't the only one concerned about Trooper's welfare. Leslie asked for email updates on his condition, and his story spread among our family of volunteers associated with the shelter.

A decision on whether to surgically repair or amputate the leg had to wait until the dog stood a better chance of survival.

The next few days depended entirely on Trooper's will to live.

People? pestered me for updates on Trooper's condition, and the vet's receptionist was being inundated with phone calls requesting information. I blasted an email to our interested well wishers, promising regular updates if they would stop calling.

Trooper's new fan club rejoiced at the news the following day when his condition improved slightly. The day after, we all cheered when we learned he could drink water.

One especially sobering concern involved how his head lolled and pitched without warning. If he couldn't even control the movements of his head, how could this dog ever have quality of life?

As we fretted, slowly but surely, Trooper regained better control of his head. Not long after, he started eating solid food. Eventually, he sat up without help, but only stood with assistance. The staff at Crestview cheered every accomplishment, along with his growing fan club.

Then his steady, almost daily improvement came to a screeching halt. Trooper reached a plateau. And he still couldn't walk. Days passed. Dr. McGruder grew more and more concerned. The dog had progressed so well, until now. He wondered why the dog couldn't stand by itself.

To make matters worse, Trooper began to show signs of fear aggression during treatments and examinations. His new behavior raised major concern. He snapped and snarled at Dr. McGruder. I worried the efforts to save Trooper had been in vain, now that the dog demonstrated potential behavioral problems.

Without access to the dog's history, for all we knew, he could have been feral before the car ran over him. All our efforts might have been wasted.

It was also possible he could have been friendly prior to the brain injury, but the trauma changed his personality.

Yet a third possibility existed: the dog might simply still be sore. His therapy could be causing him pain.

Dr. McGruder warned his staff to be careful handling the dog. Gradually, Trooper calmed and his attitude toward people improved. He licked the palm of his handler when the opportunity arose, and the display of affection encouraged all of us.

Meanwhile, Leslie went door-to-door through the neighborhood near where the dog had been injured, searching in vain for his owner. She finally found a homeowner who claimed he saw the dog running loose and put out food for it to eat. However, he said the dog remained skittish and refused to be caught.

The neighbor speculated that Trooper's previous owners dumped him like useless junk near the entrance to the subdivision. There he waited in vain for their return, until the fateful accident.

Leslie blistered my ear telling me what she learned. She made a sincere effort to find Trooper's owners, and felt certain he had been purposefully abandoned.

Dr. McGruder started to suspect Trooper's inability to stand might be related to his life prior to the accident. He could have been an outside dog. That would explain his inability to stand on slick indoor tile flooring. He carried Trooper outside. The terse but wise vet was right. Trooper stood on grass without assistance, even with his leg in a splint.

Two long weeks passed while Trooper gradually improved. Although he still required additional care, the vet believed recovery in a home environment would be more comfortable. Plus, the dog needed socialization, and it would save our Humane Society precious funds that could be used to help other animals.

As a precautionary measure, I decided Trooper should temporarily come into my home for further evaluation of potential behavioral challenges.

Finally Trooper left the hospital go home—my home. My husband has experience working with dog behavioral issues and he agreed to evaluate Trooper.

The rest of his recovery would be up to him.

When my husband, John, first met Trooper at Crestview, the frightened dog barked at him continuously. John calmly sat on the floor, refraining from eye contact with the dog. That allowed Trooper to become comfortable in his presence. After some time, Trooper inched close enough to gently sniff John's head. When Dr. McGruder joined them, the dog jumped to his side and clung to his leg like a small child.

Dr. McGruder frowned. "It may be best to have a veterinary technician the dog trusts help you get him into your car."

As he drove home, John wondered how he would get the dog with a questionable reputation *out* of his car without being bitten. He called me to discuss the problem. "I had help getting the dog into the car, but I hadn't thought of making a plan for getting him out of car." John chuckled. "I guess I don't need to worry about the dog running away. With his splinted let slowing him down, I can outrun him if he tries to escape."

Any worries about receiving a serious bite from the little dog vanished on the way home. About halfway there, the dog inched close enough to rest his muzzle on John's elbow perched on the arm rest.

John called me back to report the latest development. "I seriously doubt Trooper is going to be a problem."

"Why do you say that?"

"He's a little love bug. He's snuggling with me."

Trooper acclimated and relaxed in his new environment. He demonstrated a strong desire for affection. John believed the dog had never been wild or feral, just neglected and underappreciated. The dog was so adorable and his story heart-rending, we both felt confident Trooper would attract a lot of interest when ready and well enough to attend adoption events.

During the long weekend spent with John and our dog pack, Trooper showed zero aggression for food, people, or other dogs. His scars only made him more interesting. He house-trained easily, never once having an "accident" indoors.

I passed the good news along the volunteer grapevine -- Trooper received great reviews on his evaluation! A collective sigh of relief could be heard throughout Forsyth County.

After a long weekend of behavior evaluation, I took Trooper back to Crestview to have his injured leg re-evaluated. After his examination, we drove to meet someone very special. I let Trooper out of my van. His first steps gravitated toward the strange house, but tentatively. Leslie came outside to greet us. She took one look at Trooper and melted, saying, "Oh, Trooper!"

The emotion in her voice drew him. He hobbled to her side, tail wagging furiously, giving his best effort to leap for joy. Though he'd never gained consciousness the night she rescued him, he seemed to recognize her voice. Tears welled in Leslie's eyes at the sight of how well Trooper's recovery had progressed. I felt really good about having committed Humane Society resources to help save this dog.

With a bittersweet passing of the baton, I left the heroic little dog with Leslie. She asked to be his foster and earned the right as the one who picked his broken body off the street. As I drove away, I couldn't help but wonder if Trooper had already found his forever home. Only time would tell.

So, how many lives does a dog have? If he could answer, Trooper would surely say at least two. The best was saved for last.

Triumph Tale Desserts

The Dog That Lived Under Grandma's Bed
By John Leonard

After my wife and I fostered a dozen or more dogs for our local Humane Society, I thought we had run the gamut of dealing with difficult dog behavior. We learned how to house train puppies and older dogs that lived in the yard for years with equal success. We fostered fear-aggressive and dominance-aggressive dogs alike. We cared for laid back dogs and hyperactive ones, puppies and older dogs whose owner either died or got too sick to keep them. I was wrong to think I'd seen it all. I found this out when Lisa brought Pancho home.

I stifled a laugh, seeing Pancho for the first time. He looked as if someone painted a basset hound the colors of Rin Tin Tin. The next door neighbor's German shepherd mated with his basset hound mother; the genetic combination gave Pancho an abnormally large head upon a basset hound body, colored with the classic black-and-tan coat of his shepherd father.

But I saw that the dog acted as if he suffered. Lisa shared with me that Pancho came in with his siblings. "When he first arrived at the shelter, a puppy with his siblings, Pancho behaved like any other puppy. As people adopted his brothers, his personality grew withdrawn. I'm fairly certain that no one mistreated him at the shelter. The puppies were so young — he couldn't have been abused beforehand, either. It's just the chaos of the shelter that upsets him so much." Some dogs don't thrive in a shelter environment. Lisa recognized that with Pancho, so she brought him home.

I learned techniques to handle dogs that demonstrate aggression problems. Fear aggression isn't much different from withdrawal, which is like passive fear. I thought this would be easy to turn around. I had no idea the most difficult dog to help would be one afraid of his own shadow.

When Pancho first arrived at our house, he resisted leaving his crate. I opened the kennel door and went outside the house, leaving the exterior door open. It took some time, but he ventured out. But the dog skittered as far from me as possible, maintaining sight of his safe haven. He did his business and shot back into his kennel.

I used every technique I could recall to break through Pancho's defenses, but the dog rebuffed my every effort and distanced himself from accepting my love. With most dogs, sitting outside their kennel and ignoring them for a while would have been enough to rouse their curiosity. Not Pancho. With a little patience and a good book to pass the time, a new dog would overcome fear and come close, sniffing around, just by sheer curiosity. Pancho stayed glued to the opposite side of the kennel, as far away from human contact as possible.

The phrase *misery loves company* rang in my ears, sort of an inspiration. I felt sorry for Pancho. I began to dwell on anything that would make me miserable, driving out any thoughts of happiness, and this led to a connection with the miserable dog. Three days passed. Pancho found some bravado and ventured near the door of his kennel as I sat in the same room with a show of sadness. Bribery... I wondered if he liked peanut butter like my other dogs. I gave them medicine smeared with a gob of peanut butter and they wouldn't even know I fooled them.

I held a spoon over my shoulder through the bars of the kennel, my back turned toward him. Pancho took a taste, very reluctantly, but then cleaned the spoon. Thereafter I gave him his bribe off my fingers, blending my scent with good things like food. I didn't want to push him into retreat, so I was content that he ate peanut butter from my fingers, inserted between the bars of the kennel, for another two days. On the third day I opened the kennel door and dealt with Pancho, no protective barrier between us. I certainly didn't want to drag him out of the kennel, but I couldn't let him cower in there much longer. The bond between us came with persistence, but it grew.

Dogs are by nature pack animals. They recognize the difference between a human being and another dog. Dogs know they are dogs, but most want to be treated like people. Pancho proved to be an exception — he didn't want to act like a human being or be with people. He had little use for most humans, but Pancho really loved other dogs. His rehabilitation accelerated after we integrated him with the rest of our dog pack. I don't remember him ever meeting another dog he didn't like.

Pancho finally decided to tolerate me, and he loved my wife, but he barked at our son every time he saw him. He was an equal opportunist when it came to showing fear of tall people, short people, grandmothers, and babies. He didn't discriminate based on race, creed, gender, color, religion or national origin. He shied from just about every human being he saw.

Because our granddaughter Ava Grace had difficulty remembering the names of all the dogs that came and left our home, she called Pancho *the dog that lives under Grandma's bed.*

As soon as Pancho laid eyes on Ava, especially younger brother Ashton, he ran under our bed and remained there for the rest of their visit. Our grandchildren lived several hundred miles away, so they usually stayed with us for the whole weekend, and Pancho stayed under the bed for the whole weekend.

Dogs came to us and were adopted. Pancho got along with everybody canine. I will always remember with fondness how he chased the beagle Freckles all over our house, and how they both curled together into the smallest ball possible and slept on our bed. The memory of the basset hound Rufus always brings a smile, rollicking with Pancho and flattening a bed of liriope. My favorite memory remains Pancho lying on his back on top of my bed, writhing in pleasure, while I rubbed his belly, because he let me.

Pancho's affections seemed limited to the two of us. As foster dogs came and went, we realized that Pancho would stay a permanent member of our family. Our son Matt heard his baying objections every single day as he braved the trip upstairs; Pancho never warmed up to him. Saying that the dog feared Matt would be an understatement; the poor thing was so petrified of him that he frequently lost control of his bladder or bowels upon sight. The dog lived just a few steps from abject terror all day long. Of course, we couldn't ask our teenage son to move out, and Pancho had nowhere else to go but back to the shelter. Thank goodness for easy-to-clean wood floors.

After almost a year without an inquiry, a young woman sent Lisa an email, asking about Pancho's availability. "I grew up with basset hound mixed breeds. Your description of his special needs in the Petfinder advertisement I saw on the internet appealed to me." Reviewing her application, we hoped that she and Pancho would be a match. Lisa asked me to go along with her and help her make the decision.

He lived with us for so long; we both wanted to be sure he would be happy in his new home. We arrived at her apartment with mixed feelings, for Pancho to find his place in this world, but also for him not to go into just any home. He'd been through a lot, even now would act threatened by strangers.

A young soft-spoken woman with a kind manner greeted us. My wife and I both liked her. We were amazed to see Pancho relax in her presence as he met her. The dog set out and explored her apartment. I slipped the young woman a bag of his favorite treats, convinced she'd need them as bribes. Pancho ventured near enough to meet her. She sealed the deal for his affection at every brave approach with a treat. His drive by sniffs grew more frequent, easily taking what she offered. I felt a pang of jealousy to see how easily he took food from her when it had been so difficult for me.

The last thing Lisa wanted to happen was for Pancho to accept his new home and regress to behavior his new owner couldn't accept. We spent time and disclosed his history in detail, not the least of which, his reaction to young teenage boys. The young woman smiled brightly. "No worries. I teach high school, so I'm not crazy about teenage boys, either." We shared a laugh, an instant common denominator for bonding.

Pancho had finally found a home where he would never again have to live under the bed.

Cisco

By Amy E. Zajac

Snow blew into drifts higher than I'd ever seen. I looked out the window. A large drift blanketed the whole side of the car in the driveway since breakfast. *Nine o'clock. I can't believe we'll get to move to our new house today.* "Everything looks frozen, Mom. Are you sure we can move today?"

"Today's the only day we can do it. It will be okay."

I didn't believe what Mom told me. "After I finish washing the breakfast dishes, what do you want me to do?"

"Is your bedroom completely packed?"

"Yeah, Mom." *She knows that.*

"Okay, you keep track of the cats. We can't risk that Cisco or Poncho will escape outside in this weather. They need to stay away from the trucks, in and out of the drive."

"When can we take them to the new house?" Impatience escaped my mouth as I watched from the window. Flakes piled higher by the minute.

"They'll go with us on our last trip, tonight."

"So I have to stay here all day ... and take care of them?"

"That's right. I don't want to worry about them getting loose."

My stomach knotted up. If I complained, I'd get in trouble. I wanted to go back and forth with everyone else. *Not fair.* I looked over at Poncho and Cisco, inseparable as always, as they sat on the window sill in the dining room, fascinated watching the snowfall. *I need to think of a way to get over to the new house, at least once before tonight. I know. Lunch!*

"Hey, Mom, can I go over on the lunch run?"

"Yes. Now stop bothering me! I have to finish the packing. Your Dad will be back with a truck in a little while."

Everything started to roll when Dad got home with the borrowed truck. A few of his friends arrived to help. The morning bustled by, everyone emptying furniture and boxes, room after room. Noon came. Mom told me to dress extra warm and ride with her to the new house, only a mile and a half away. On a good weather day the trip would take a few minutes. The ride took 20 minutes in the storm, as the car skidded in spots when Mom accelerated. Snow plows didn't service either our old or new street, so Mom inched forward in tire tracks made by other cars. The windshield wipers sounded muffled, like we were buried in snow.

After a great lunch with hot chocolate, sandwiches, and the donuts leftover from breakfast, Mom and I headed back to our old house, because she needed to direct our friends about what and how to move our furniture. *And I'll be stuck cat sitting for a very long afternoon.*

When we walked in, Poncho sat across from the door, awaiting our arrival. Cisco was not with her. *That's strange.* I shed my boots, shook snow off my coat, and hung it up. Poncho watched me. "Cisco, where are you?" He didn't come out of hiding. I looked in all their usual places, but no Cisco. I got a creeping feeling that Cisco got outside, somehow. My stomach knotted up. I broke into a cold sweat. *What am I going to tell Mom?*

Mom stood before me, her hands on her hips, flames out of her eyes, but she let me go outside to look for Cisco. I knew she wanted me out from under foot. Poncho knew to stay out of everyone's way, curled up into a ball in a corner of the dining room.

I yelled and yelled for Cisco, but he never showed. While I looked for him, I started to enjoy the snow. The wind blew hard and toppled me into snowdrifts. I was snow covered. So it was just the right time to make snow angels, as I looked for my little friend. After a while I sat in a snow bank to rest.

"Amy, get back into the house!" Mom yelled from the garage. "You'll get sick. You're all wet. And look, your lips are turning blue! Why do you always stay out so long and get so cold? I just don't know why you do that!"

"But Mom, Cisco is out here all alone. He'll get stuck in the snow. I have to keep looking. And besides I don't feel cold. I'm warm."

"Cisco will find a place to hide. We'll call him in, later. Just get in here and take off your wet clothes."

Wrapped up in a cozy blanket, Poncho and I watched out the window through the afternoon. The storm buried the mounds formed earlier in the day. New falling snow soon covered my tracks and all my snow angels. Cisco didn't come home.

Before we left for the new house that night, Mom went outside and called for Cisco many times. He usually came when we called his name, but this time he didn't. The wind whistled through the metal gutters, frozen over with icicles from the last storm. Mom's voice evaporated into the wind, snow, and darkness. "Amy, we have to leave. We'll come back tomorrow and look for him."

"But he'll freeze. We can't just leave him." I stood my ground to protect my little friend, not knowing what to do, but I never planned to give up.

"We'll come back tomorrow." Mom looked away.

Tears ran down my cheeks. I wiped them away with my jacket sleeve. I sobbed all the way to the new house as I gripped Poncho too tight. He squirmed to get away from me, but I wouldn't let him go. I held him firmly in my arms.

The snow plows took several days to dig through the accumulation, just in time for another storm to hit us. Mom and Dad drove to the old house many times, even in the new snowstorm. They didn't find Cisco. I missed him every morning. He would always be on the end of my bed when I woke up. I could tell, Poncho missed him, too. He and I spent that week getting used to the new house. We discovered many new corners and hiding places.

The sixth morning after the move, the sun shone through the window and startled me. I heard water as it dripped off the roof and formed new icicles. Our new house differed a lot from the old one. These very long icicles reminded me of swords from the pirate stories I read recently, following the roof line single file along the whole side of the house that faced the morning sun.

I helped shovel snow later in the afternoon. It crunched under my feet while the cold wind burned my cheeks. So we didn't have to lift too much snow because it was deep and heavy, we made very narrow walkways. I loved this activity after a week stuck inside, so many days that school was called off. According to my mother, once again I stayed outside much longer than I should. I trudged in through the back door of the enclosed porch, which adjoined the kitchen. My fingers were numb, hard to hang my wet clothes on the hooks by the door. I cleaned up just in time for dinner. We all sat to eat together, my sister, my parents, and me.

After a couple minutes, I thought I heard something. "Shhh! Listen! Is Poncho meowing? He must have slipped out the back porch when we came in."

Mom went out to the porch to let him in. "Poncho's not out here!"

We all rose from the table, because the meowing got louder.

"I think it's coming from outside." Mom opened the door. Cold wind blew inside. Dad turned the spot-light on. I rushed to the outer door and looked. *How in the world–* In the shadows at the bottom of the outside stairs I saw Cisco. Icy pellets hung on his long matted fur all the way to the ground. He appeared wild and acted skittish.

We called him in. Cisco pranced up the stairs into the porch as if we just let him out ten minutes before. We fed him and dried him off. When I picked him up, I could tell he lost a lot of weight over the week. Poncho greeted him; they bumped heads in their usual habit. Cisco followed Poncho to other rooms, explored, and made himself right at home.

It took seven days, but Cisco found his way to rejoin his family through two snow storms. Somehow, he found a house where he'd never been before, but he knew we were inside. The cat literally called to us to open the door and let him come home.

Memphis and the Mighty Ox
By John Leonard

My wife Lisa became overwhelmed with compassion when she saw Memphis and his pathetic mental disposition. She only needed a way to make me aware of his plight. A medium-sized Australian shepherd mix, afraid of his own shadow, someone had to place him into a forever home before the effects of institutionalization did permanent damage. Originally adopted from the Humane Society as a puppy, the dog lived a happy life with his family for more than six years. When their youngest child left for college, the parents decided they no longer had time to spend with Memphis. They gave him back to the Humane Society.

Lisa sensed he needed a stable and loving foster environment and wanted to bring him home. With a hidden agenda that I learned later, she walked me through the dog kennel area, so I would see how pitiful Memphis appeared. While this community shelter didn't euthanize animals, which was their policy, this dog never lived with another dog. He lived in an enclosed kennel in a large building with a cacophony of barking dogs, huddled in the far recesses of his run, shaking in fright. The dog left with us when we went home.

His first attempt to adapt to a foster home failed miserably. The newcomer quickly grew jealous of the permanent dog in the home and showed minor signs of aggression. The foster caregiver brought Memphis back to the shelter where he quickly became a nervous wreck. He did not know how to interact with other canines or acclimate to their presence.

We have an established dog pack in our home that Lisa calls *the core four*: Shiloh, a large black and tan German Shepherd that we permanently foster due to his medical issues; Gracie, the queen who rules the roost; Rusty, an older collie-mix, a mama's boy; and the unchallenged leader of the pack, Ox. A giant solid black German Shepherd, he's about 95 pounds of solid muscle. When Memphis temporarily joined our family, he attempted to assert himself as alpha dog, usurping Ox's place at my heel. That did not bode well for his life expectancy. Most dogs fostered at our home developed social skills to understand their place in a dog pack. They all enjoy the freedom of roaming the yard and exploring our home, released from their former shelter restrictions, but they all know beyond doubt, Lisa and I are pack leaders. Ox was the first dog I rescued and adopted, and he's fiercely devoted to me. He's also twice the size of Memphis.

Memphis had not spent much time in the great outdoors. He went outside to do his business if a human being accompanied him, but he acted afraid outside the house. As soon as he finished his call of nature, Memphis zipped inside, unlike the rest of our pack. Lisa compared his personality to TV's Adrian Monk — *it's a jungle out there.*

Despite these quirks of behavior, Memphis challenged Ox as pack leader. Their first fight began and ended within a few seconds. Memphis attacked Ox without provocation and suffered dire consequences. Ox defended himself without injury, actually restraining himself as he caused Memphis only minor damage, a small bloody cut above his eyes. But this was not the end of his challenge. Memphis never attacked any of the other dogs, only Ox, as if he had a death wish. The bigger dog put his attacker in his proper place, using amazing restraint, and he never settled the fights like I knew he could.

Memphis often lost control and attacked Ox when he got excited, for instance, if company came to the house or Lisa had dinner cooking. He worked himself into a frenzy, racing in circles around the tables and through the kitchen, barking and yelping with reckless abandon. Most of these episodes escalated, and he snapped at Ox, and the smaller dog always fared worse than his intended victim. These skirmishes grew more and more frequent.

One night at dinner Memphis lost control attacked Ox once more. The rest of the pack cleared space for the two dogs to square off. When I restrained Ox by his collar, Lisa yelled, "Let Ox go! He can't defend himself. Memphis is the aggressor."

I let go and grabbed my handy tennis racquet, an excellent "wedge" tool to separate two dogs without hurting them or suffering dog bite. Ox charged forward and knocked Memphis down. He rolled Memphis onto his back and grabbed the smaller dog's throat in his jaws. A single bite, Memphis would be dead. I believe that both animals realized this. They got quiet. Ox removed his mouth but used his giant paw to keep him pinned to the ground. He towered over him and glared into his eyes, like he dared Memphis to move. Ox had enough of this nonsense. The fight ended. Decisively and without question, Ox emerged, the victor.

After that confrontation Memphis mellowed in character and attitude. He accepted his place in our house and the love we offered. The healing process began, leading Memphis into a new life as a happier dog among canine and human alike.

Ditto and Bogart
By Amy E. Zajac

After I lived in my new house for a couple of weeks, two stray cats showed up outside my patio door. They rubbed back and forth at the patio window as if they were saying hello. I saw that these cats knew each other by their playful antics. They licked each other faces, rolled over each other, gnawing at the other's neck, not really fighting. One, basically white with large gray spots, a solid build and no tail, dominated the other smaller cat, with a long gray-fur-coat and striking slanted eyes. The gray acted aloof, probably the elder.

Over the next few days I placed dry cat food outside my back door. Although I never saw my new friends eating, the food disappeared. Early on the fourth morning, my doorbell rang. Donna, the former owner of my house stood and smiled at me.

"Hello, Donna. This *is* a surprise. Please come in."

"Hi, Amy. I'm sorry to disturb you so early, but I needed to stop over before I went to work."

"Not a problem, I've been getting up early to unpack and settle in."

"My cats are missing. We brought them with us, the last day we moved out. They stayed in our garage for a day, but when the thunderstorms started, we brought them into the house. With the new surroundings and the storm, the two were skittish and uneasy. They snuck out of the house about two weeks ago. I tried to get them back in, but they slipped away into the weeds in the vacant lot near the pond on our new property. I saw them the next day, but after that, I didn't see them again. I hoped, by some miracle, they'd be here. I know cats sometimes go back to their former homes when they get uprooted like this."

"Yes, I think they're here. I didn't know whose cats they were. I've been feeding them out back for about four days. How far is it to your house?"

"A mile and a half. Can you believe it? It's so amazing." Donna relaxed and let out a sigh.

"It is amazing. What are their names?"

"Ditto and Bogart."

"Which one is Ditto?" I became curious, because they were so cute.

"The white and gray one; he has no tail, because I accidentally ran over it with my car a couple years ago. I rushed him to the vet, who amputated it to keep away infection."

"That's so sad. But he doesn't seem to mind."

"Ditto's a great cat. After he healed from the surgery, he was just fine. Do you know where they are right now? I'd like to take them home." Donna smiled broadly and jumped up on her toes to look around.

"My bet is that they're by my patio door."

"Yes, that's their place."

We walked through the house to the patio door. "I noticed, Bogart looks pretty skinny. He's eaten some since he's been back here. I believe the trip finding the house took its toll on him."

"Thanks so much for feeding them. I do appreciate it."

There they were. Ditto and Bogart basked in the sunshine on the back stoop. Donna expressed her gratitude and took them home.

The rest of the day, I finished unpacking. My next priority, I decided to settle in a bit, then check out my new yard. With so much acreage the day's work in the garden spread into weeks. What I needed to accomplish in the yard I planned to complete just prior to the heat of summer. As I started on the holly bushes in the front yard, I discovered Bogart next to the larger bush, sunning and having a great June afternoon. .

"What are you doing here? I eased up next to him and bent over to pat him. He allowed me. "Is your friend with you?" My fingertips traced his extended ribs. His fur was full of burrs. "Bogart, you must be so uncomfortable." As I moved a burr over, he jerked away and scurried toward the woods at the back of my house. I spotted Ditto as a flash of white. They both disappeared into the underbrush.

Sure they were hungry; I placed some food out on the stoop. I called Donna to let her know Ditto and Bogart were here. Once again, Donna took her two cats home and I went back into my new routine on the hill. Summer set in. I enjoyed my new house with all its beauty and its added work. And Ditto and Bogart returned to our hilltop again. I called Donna who picked them up after work.

About three weeks later Donna rang my doorbell. "Hi Amy. Have you seen my boys? They've been gone for a while, so I figured they came here."

"No, I haven't seen them."

"I just want you to know, Amy, I believe Ditto and Bogart are your cats, now. They belong here, it seems. I won't be coming back for them anymore."

"Are you sure, Donna? They're so sweet. You've had them for quite a while."

"Yes, I'm sure. I love them, but hunting for them when they run off is very hard, with my new baby to care for. I thought this out logically. I hope you understand. The cats both seem to prefer living here. When we spoke before, you sounded as if you liked them."

"Yes, I sure do. I guess they adopted me, because it's their house and I come with it." I laughed and Donna joined me. " I'm sure it will be a good solution for us all."

"I appreciate your understanding and that you're willing to take care of them."

"No problem. I've never had outdoor cats before. I'll have to watch out for them. They could be here already, and I just haven't seen them yet."

"Please call me if you have any questions." Donna flashed a large smile as she left.

A whole week passed by before I saw them. Ditto lay stretched out on my back stoop as I rounded the corner of the house to pull some weeds. I saw the food I left there was gone. I looked around searching the perimeter of the woods. *No Bogart.* Moving closer to Ditto, I gently patted his back. "How are you doing, Ditto? I guess from now on you'll be mine." I think he actually understood what I told him. Barely moving, he purred and let me pat his stomach.

Bogart showed up for food later that day. We settled into a pattern. When I worked outside, they followed me from task to task. I enjoyed their company.

A couple months passed. One evening as I lay on the couch with my two indoor cats, both dozing, I glanced out the back window. Ditto gazed in through the patio door and stared at us. *Oh Ditto, don't look so sad. My cats always lived indoors. They were never outdoor cats.* I went out to the back stoop and sat down with Ditto, and gazed into the woods. After that day, Ditto waited every evening for me to sit with him. Bogart showed up just once in a while. But this became Ditto's time. My two indoor cats sat behind us every night, peering at us through the patio door window.

Simon/Simone
By John Leonard

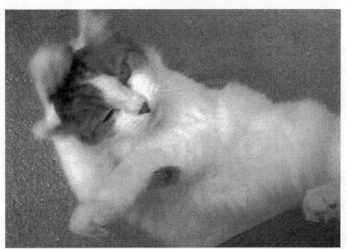

One night our son Matt found an abandoned cat outside the Humane Society as he closed for the night. The cat had been secured inside a pet carrier left next to the front door. Matt called the cat Simon; the name was neatly printed in block letters on a piece of tape that adorned the carrier door. Because the cat had been abandoned with no veterinary records, Matt had to bring Simon home. He knew that unvaccinated strays posed a risk to cats already housed at the shelter. The two rounds of shots required a ten day quarantine period as part of the protocol.

When Matt came home with this cat, which caused a great deal of interest in our house, they rushed upstairs away from the rest of the household. We are a dog pack family; the pack in unison vociferously protested the addition of a feline. Even worse than the barking, the dogs milled at the bottom of the stairs, silently waiting for the moment the cat made his fatal mistake, following curiosity to its logical conclusion.

None of us dared to investigate pack motives; it seemed we made a good decision, separating the cat and the dogs, until Simon was placed in a good home. I installed two baby gates on our stairwell, which blocked off the bedrooms from the living area. A gate placed at the bottom prevented the dogs from coming upstairs, and the second gate at the top served as an additional defensive barrier. Simon had the run of the upstairs, and the dogs ruled the downstairs. Actually, because of my allergies and because I had no reason to bond with the cat, Simon stayed in the guest bedroom.

Released from his carrier, I noticed that Simon appeared an attractive long-haired cat with a distinctive tabby mask and tail. His beautiful long white fur made it impossible for me to spot any surgical scars and confirm that he had been neutered. I made a surgical appointment with the vet for a complete exam. A couple of days later, Simon went under the knife. A very perplexed vet called us a few hours later, letting me know Simon was a female cat. The neuter procedure changed to a spay surgery, mid-operation. The vet then discovered Simon, now named Simone by necessity, had undergone a full hysterectomy.

The indignity of the belly shave, the effects of the anesthesia, and the needless surgery made Simone one grumpy cat. I took some pity on her and allowed her out to visit the other upstairs bedrooms. She seemed fond of Matt's room, perhaps, because she recognized him as her rescuer, and began to hang out there. Matt learned more about her personality, telling us every one of his discoveries. One day he said, "Simone thinks she's a dog!"

I asked him what he meant.

"When the rest of the dogs barked at the garbage truck, Simone joined in, growling just like she was one of them!"

I laughed along, not sure if Matt was serious. and chalked it up as the vivid imagination of a bored college student. Our son worked two days last month, because in the slow summer economy, he couldn't find a steady job. One of those work days he brought this cat home. But, as far as cats go, he couldn't have picked a better one. After a while I changed perception. Simone didn't think she was one of the dogs. She appointed herself their queen. She would perch at the top of the stairs, impervious to the irritation and whining she roused in her subjects below, and lorded over them with calm disdain. Occasionally Simone ventured down the stairs and gave face to face affront to the pack.

I grew to see that Simone liked to follow people around, just hang out with the human beings, which seemed more like dog behavior than cat. Simone's fur didn't aggravate my allergies like other cats. I knew how attached Matt had become to the cat; we entertained thoughts we might adopt her. I had to consider that one of the big dogs could hurt this gentle soul, should she circumvent the barriers, so I had to abandon ownership for Matt and post her adoption information on the shelter's website. We could enjoy her as a foster home, but her best option for a forever home did not include life among a pack of large dogs.

Simone had a personality unlike any other cat I'd ever known. Her demeanor was very unique. Her manner was friendly, without a hostile bone in her body, and she never demanded attention, but she always stood aloof. I could read her emotions like a book. When I tried to pick her up, though I gripped her at both side securely, she tried to escape and gave a look I could see that she didn't want to be held. When I lifted her, she'd squirm a little and then go limp as a rag doll. I knew that once her efforts, halfhearted it seemed, proved futile, she made the most of it, started purring and settled in.

Lisa and I cataloged her eccentric behavior and compared notes. She researched the internet and identified these unusual characteristics as associated with a type called *the rag doll cat*. Simone appeared to be a textbook example of a rag doll. Her only characteristic that didn't match the prototypical description of the breed were her amber eyes; they would typically appear blue.

An older couple submitted an application and seemed to be a perfect match for Simone. The couple decided to open their home to a new cat after grieving for their deceased pet. These folks proved they were the right choice and their home would be great for Simone. But we now faced a challenge. How could we let someone else adopt this wonderful cat with whom the entire family — except the dogs — fell in love?

Fostering has bittersweet rewards.

Left Behind
By Donna Sundblad

  It didn't thrill me to move from the country to the city, but our family had outgrown our house. Since we needed to move, my parents decided to cut time off Dad's commute and relocate closer to Chicago. At age 12 it seemed to me we planned to leave behind everything I knew and loved.

  By the time our two bedroom house sold, Mom was close to delivering baby number seven. That's why we had to move. Two bedrooms, one bath and seven kids equaled organized chaos, and my parents were tired of sleeping on the hide-a-bed.

  The new house provided more than enough room. Our sofa, two over-stuffed chairs, and tables didn't even fill half the new living room. I liked having a fireplace, but I wondered if this new "old" house could ever feel like home. When I say old, I mean plaster walls, arched doorways, crown molding, and even a coal delivery door, from the days when coal heated the house. Even with the door soldered shut and a modern gas furnace, the basement gave me the creeps.

  The basement stretched from one room, where the laundry sinks hung, to a second room with a workbench and the furnace. The people who moved out left all kinds of junk, old tools, furniture, an antique iron, cast iron utensils — it gave me a queasy feeling, like something lurked in the shadows. Flimsy wainscoting walls enclosed a half bath. The door latched with a hook and eye. Inside the half-bath a large bin hung, with double doors to catch dirty clothes thrown down the laundry chute. Everything was just so... different. And old.

  When the departing family turned over the keys, the mother mentioned they had lost a hamster in the house. "It's been over a month since we've seen it," she said. "It must have gotten outside."

  "What's a hamster?" my mom asked Dad.

Dad shrugged. "It doesn't matter. It's gone."

The two of them looked around our new house, their faces so happy. How could they not miss our old house? Our friends?

Our chores expanded with the bigger house. I used to like running diapers through the ringers on the washer in our old house, but not anymore. I dreaded working in the new basement. Mom understood. She walked down the stairs with her big belly leading the way. I felt guilty because diapers had to be washed every other day.

One day Mom headed down the stairs with the diaper hamper. I stood in the kitchen struggling with guilt and the thought that I should be helping her. A bloodcurdling scream from the basement shattered my preoccupation. *Mom!* I scurried down the first few stairs. *Mom's having the baby!* I bent and peeked through the opening where the stairwell wall ended and the railing started — just in case a monster or murderer hid. No intruders. And Mom wasn't having the baby. She stood three feet from the washing machine with her hands clasped in front of her.

I bounded down the rest of the stairs to the cracked cement floor. "What's wrong, Mom?

She pointed a shaky finger. "There's a mouse in the sink! A mouse!"

I rushed to the large twin laundry sinks. "It's not a mouse, Mom. Wrong color. It looks like its tail has been cut off. I bet it's the hamster. I'll get it." I paused to study the cute golden critter standing on its hind legs at the bottom of the sink. Mom acted like it was a monster! I nearly laughed, but I knew better.

I scrounged up an empty box and a pencil while Mom rushed upstairs. With the eraser end and prodded the little critter toward the box. It spun and snapped like the Tasmanian Devil. I jerked back. *No wonder the people didn't care they left this behind.* I touched the eraser to the hamster's back and it jumped again.

This time it landed over the box's cardboard flap. In a flash I tipped it and lifted the little animal from the sink. "Gotcha!"

As I walked up the stairs, I admired the soft-looking golden fur. My foot crossed the threshold into the kitchen. Mom stopped me. "Take that thing back into the basement! I don't want it up here."

Sheesh, she acts like I'm trying to bring a snake in the house. I knew better than to argue and turned to head back down the stairs. The hamster curled up into a ball in the corner. I sat on the cold basement floor and watched it. *What will I name it?* I tried to stroke it with the pencil. It shot to life and snapped, revealing a flash of its two very long teeth. I touched it again and again and talked to it. Gradually, it relaxed and finally ignored my touch. Its little nose twitched. Long whiskers stretched from its snout like antennae that brushed the side of the box. "Whiskers would be a good name," I said. "Too common. Whiskey? No, that isn't right. How about Winky?"

I mustered my courage and put the pencil down. It was time to touch it with my finger. My heart raced. Mom will kill me if it bites me. I licked my dry lips and reached into the box, still talking in a quiet voice. "What do you think of Winky?" I asked as if it would answer. My finger brushed its velvety golden fur. It jumped, but didn't spin or try to bite me. I touched it again and let my finger linger. After about an hour, I held Winky in the palm of my hand. It stepped from one hand to another without stopping, like an endless flights of stairs. On much closer examination, I saw my new bundle of fur was a female.

Mom and Dad decided I could keep Winky. We all went to a store and bought her a small cage. It didn't take long before I discovered how Winky escaped in the first place. She unlatched the hook that locked the door. I wired it shut. She learned to push the tray in the bottom of the cage forward enough to slip out. I stared at the empty cage heartbroken. Worse yet, I had to tell Mom Winky was loose in the house, again.

We searched everywhere. Mom delivered the bad news. "I heard the hamster in our bedroom wall," she said to Dad.

Winky had climbed into a hole in the back of the second floor linen closet and fallen to the first floor. With my hamster trapped in the wall between the bedroom and half bath on the first floor, my parents tried to console me. *Winky is trapped in the wall without food or water. She could die.*

I went into my parent's bedroom and talked through the wall, just to let her know she wasn't alone. A little scratching noise tore at my heart. *I had to get her out of there, but how? They would never let me make a hole in the wall.*

I went down to the basement and looked at the wood lathe ceiling. The plumbing helped me figure out where Winky might be. I climbed into the clothes chute bin and listened. A faint scratching helped me determine where to make a hole. *It wouldn't have to be a big hole. A hamster can fit through an amazingly small crack.* I went to Dad's tool bench, grabbed a hammer and large screwdriver. Little by little, I chiseled a hole into the basement ceiling and opened it to the size of a dime. I ran upstairs and grabbed a carrot from the refrigerator. I stuck the tip into the hole and felt a tug. "Winky!" The tip of the carrot broke off. I could just imagine her munching away on that moist sweet carrot. At least she was still alive. I needed to make the hole bigger.

The pounding brought Dad into the basement. "What are you doing?"

Hands overhead holding his tools, I looked down at him from inside the laundry bin. I thought for sure he'd kill me. "Winky is alive, Dad. She took part of a carrot I stuck in there."

"Don't make that hole bigger than a quarter. That should be plenty big enough to get her out."

His footsteps disappeared up the stairs, and I let out a sigh, thankful that he understood. I chiseled and chipped the hard wood overhead and stuck the carrot back in the hole. Winky tugged it. I pulled it free and let it rest just outside the opening. Her little nose and whiskers appeared. I needed something that wouldn't break off as easily as the carrot. I headed back to the refrigerator and rummaged through the crisper drawer. "Ah-ha! Celery." I pulled off a stalk and hurried back to the half-bath in the basement. Light from the window faded with the afternoon, so I pulled the string of the single bulb hanging from the ceiling. The glare cast a shadow as I climbed into the laundry bin. The celery stalk didn't quite fit—a tad too wide. I bit it, and tried again. It fit! Within seconds Winky had her teeth sunk in the celery. I pulled it away just a little. She tugged back. I wanted her to really set her bite so I could pull her out of the hole.

It worked! She wasn't about to let go. I inched the celery from the ceiling with Winky in tow. In the dim light her gray fur startled me. She looked like a mouse! Coal dust must have settled between the walls years ago! Mom would freak. I cupped her next to my chest and let her nibble the celery, which she bit off in little chunks and stored in her pouches.

I headed up the stairs, thankful our house had a basement, even a creepy one, or I would never have been able to save Winky from her trap between the walls.

Writers Alliance of Georgia Contributing Authors

Beverly Forster, a fundraiser and supporter of the Harris Arts Center in Calhoun, GA, is one of the original members of the Gordon County Writers Guild, now known as the Writers Alliance of Georgia (WAG). She lives with her husband Steve, and enjoys her two grown sons and their families who live nearby. Her delivery of humor in all her writing exemplifies her style as a storyteller. Whether domesticated or wild neighborhood inhabitants, her pet friends are all drawn to her gentle loving manner.

Angie Kinsey, a native of Nashville, TN, is a writer, blogger, and public speaker. From software manuals to fantastic fiction, Angie, spent most of her career in the corporate world writing and speaking to diverse audiences. She enjoys writing inspirational fictional and creative non-fiction stories. Her previous works include software manuals, publications in collegiate anthologies, and various articles. She currently resides in NW Georgia with her husband, Mark. She hosts a daily inspirational blog "The Newspaper for the Soul" at www.anjikinzywhimy.com, a bi-weekly blog devoted to the process of art at www.AngieKinsey.com, and is a proud member of the Writers Alliance of Georgia.

Béla M. Krusac, an educator since 1968, taught every subject from first grade through 8th grade, high school art, math, and English. He currently teaches technology and business at Georgia Northwestern Technical College. He earned his B.A. degree at Olivet College in Literature, and received a Master of Arts in Teaching from Andrews University. He developed his love of cats early, when his sister rescued a homeless kitten from the perils of the highway median. He lives in Georgia with his wife Christy and their three adopted stray cats: Pumpkin, Pokey (Old Blue Eyes) and Scaredy-Cat.

Christy Krusac, a retired elementary school teacher, spent most of her tenure teaching kindergarten. During those years learning from five and six year olds, she developed a keen ear for literature that appeals to that age. She is in the process of selecting a publisher for two picture books in their final stages. Favorite passtimes include spending time with her husband, Béla, and also with their three kindergarten-age granddaughters. Over the years, they owned two dogs and one cat that all lived to old age. Other feline friends came and went during their lifetime in Michigan and subsequently, Georgia.

John Leonard volunteers for the HSFC (Humane Society of Forsyth County) and serves on its board of directors. His book *Divine Evolution: a hybrid theory reconciling creationism and evolution* is available through his website at www.southernprose.com, where viewers can find links to his articles at *American Thinker* or writings as Atlanta Creationism Examiner. He is Vice President of the Writer's Alliance of Georgia (WAG). With his wife Lisa, they have fostered and helped adopt more than seventy animals over a three year period. Many of their temporary "houseguests" helped inspire some of the stories found in this anthology.

Donna Sundblad, a full time writer, author, writing coach, and speaker resides in NW Georgia with her husband, Rick. She serves as Atlanta Bible Study Examiner and Christian Women's Encouragement Examiner at Examiner.com, presides over the Writer's Alliance of Georgia, and facilitates an online goal-oriented study group for writers through Writer's Village University. Donna's third fantasy novel, *The Inheritance* was nominated for a 2012 Epic Award. Other published works include magazine articles, a self-help book for writers, and various inspirational short stories, including those found in *Life Savors* and *Cup of Comfort*. For more information, visit her website at http://theinkslinger.net/wp/.

Rick Sundblad lives in rural Northwest Georgia with his wife Donna and their flock of pets. Rick has written numerous devotional and discipleship pieces covering a wide variety of Christian topics published online and in print. He enjoys history and is currently working on a book related to the historical journey of the church from biblical times to the present.

Amy E. Zajac relocated to San Diego, however continues to maintain her relationship with the Writer's Alliance of Georgia (WAG). Her stories, *That Magic Moment*, published in *A Cup of Comfort for Divorced Women*, and *A Moment of Dignity*, previously published in *Pets Across America Two*, are very diverse. Several of her articles as a correspondent for the Chattanooga Times Free Press, made front page bylines. A weekly volunteer at the La Jolla Playhouse and Feeding America, San Diego, still allows her time to grow her mother's WW II biography, plus edit her first novel. She's loved a myriad of cat and dog friends since her childhood.

Contributing Guest Author
Roy Berman, a member of Writer's Village University since 1997, joined the staff of ePress-online in 2005 as an intern editor, became a lead editor for fiction and non-fiction, and was promoted to Senior Fantasy Editor. He has edited three books which were nominated for Epic eBook awards; *The Inheritance* by Donna Sundblad received a nomination for 2012. Roy is currently writing a self-help curriculum on biblical prophecy, ghostwriting pastoral teaching materials, mentoring students at Writer's Village, and crafting a humorous fantasy novel.

Made in the USA
Charleston, SC
07 September 2012